ANGER MANAGEMENT
FOR PARENTS

Integrating Philosophy, Psychology, and Theology

Dr. Maxwell Shimba

Printed by Shimba Publishing LLC
Printed in the United States of America

TABLE OF CONTENTS

INTRODUCTION

Understanding Anger and Its Impact on Parenting

Anger is a fundamental human emotion, one that arises in response to perceived threats or injustices. While it can serve as a catalyst for change and self-protection, uncontrolled anger can have detrimental effects, particularly in the context of parenting. For parents, managing anger effectively is crucial not only for their own well-being but also for the emotional health and development of their children.

In the realm of parenting, anger often manifests through stress, frustration, or feelings of helplessness. These reactions can disrupt family dynamics, lead to strained relationships, and impact a child's emotional and psychological development. Unchecked anger can undermine the nurturing environment essential for a child's growth and contribute to a cycle of negative behavior that affects all members of the family.

The Necessity of Anger Management

Effective anger management is vital for several reasons. First, it helps maintain a positive and supportive environment at home, which is fundamental for healthy family interactions. Second, it enables parents to model constructive emotional regulation for their children, teaching them valuable skills for handling their own emotions. Third, managing anger can reduce the risk of conflicts escalating into more severe issues, fostering a more harmonious and stable family life.

The challenge lies in addressing anger in a manner that is not merely reactive but proactive and reflective. This involves understanding the root causes of anger, recognizing its manifestations, and applying strategies to control and redirect it constructively.

A Comprehensive Approach: Philosophy, Psychology, and Theology

This book aims to provide a multifaceted approach to anger management by integrating insights from philosophy, psychology, and theology. Each of these disciplines offers unique perspectives and tools that can enrich our understanding of anger and enhance our ability to manage it effectively.

- Philosophy offers a rich tradition of thought on emotions, virtue, and self-control. Ancient philosophers such as Aristotle and the Stoics have contributed valuable insights into the nature of anger and its management. Their teachings emphasize the importance of cultivating virtues like patience and wisdom, which can help temper anger and guide it towards constructive outcomes.

- Psychology provides empirical research and practical strategies for understanding and managing anger. By examining psychological theories on emotional regulation, cognitive-behavioral approaches, and stress management techniques, we can develop effective methods for controlling anger and improving emotional health.

- Theology provides spiritual and moral guidance on anger. Religious teachings often address the role of anger in human life, offering insights into its spiritual significance and ways to reconcile anger with faith and forgiveness. This perspective can help parents draw on their spiritual beliefs to find strength and guidance in managing their emotions.

Purpose and Structure of the Book

The goal of this book is to offer a comprehensive strategy for anger management that draws from these three disciplines. We will explore the nature of anger, its psychological underpinnings, philosophical insights into emotional control, and theological perspectives on dealing with anger. By integrating these approaches, we aim to provide parents with a holistic framework for understanding and managing their emotions effectively.

Each chapter will address a specific aspect of anger management, providing practical tools and strategies that can be applied in everyday life. We will also include real-life examples, case studies, and exercises to help parents implement these strategies and track their progress.

A Journey Toward Emotional Well-being

Managing anger is a journey that requires self-awareness, commitment, and practice. By exploring the intersections of philosophy, psychology, and theology, this book seeks to equip parents with the knowledge and tools necessary to navigate this journey. Our hope is that through this integrated approach, parents will gain a deeper understanding of their emotions, develop effective strategies for managing anger, and foster a healthier and more harmonious family environment.

In the chapters that follow, we will delve into the complexities of anger, offering practical advice and insights that will empower parents to approach their emotions with greater clarity and control. This journey toward emotional well-being is not just about managing anger but also about enriching the quality of family life and fostering a positive and nurturing environment for children.

DR. MAXWELL SHIMBA

CHAPTER 01

UNDERSTANDING ANGER

Definition and Nature of Anger

Anger is a powerful and complex emotion that every human being experience at some point in their life. It is a natural, often automatic response to perceived threats, injustices, or frustrations. While anger can serve as a protective mechanism, alerting us to potential dangers or motivating us to address wrongs, it can also become destructive when it is not managed appropriately. To fully grasp the nature of anger, it is essential to explore its definition, its physiological and psychological aspects, and the role it plays in human behavior.

Defining Anger

Anger can be defined as an emotional state that varies in intensity, from mild irritation to intense fury and rage. It is characterized by feelings of antagonism, frustration, and hostility toward someone or something perceived to have wronged or obstructed us. Anger is often categorized as a negative emotion due to its association with conflict, aggression, and other destructive behaviors. However, it is important to recognize that anger is not inherently negative; it can be a constructive force when channeled appropriately.

The American Psychological Association (APA) defines anger as "an emotion characterized by antagonism toward someone or something you feel has deliberately done you wrong." This definition highlights the relational aspect of anger, as it often arises in response to actions or situations perceived as unjust or harmful.

Anger is a universal emotion, transcending cultural, geographical, and social boundaries. It is deeply rooted in human nature and has been extensively studied in various fields, including psychology, philosophy, and theology. Understanding anger requires us to look beyond its immediate manifestations and delve into the underlying processes that trigger and sustain it.

Physiological Aspects of Anger

Anger is not just an emotional experience; it is also a physiological one. When we become angry, our bodies undergo a series of changes that prepare us for a fight-or-flight response. This reaction is deeply embedded in our evolutionary history, where anger played a crucial role in survival.

- The Role of the Brain: The brain plays a central role in the experience of anger. When a person perceives a threat or injustice, the amygdala, a part of the brain associated with emotional processing, is activated. The amygdala then sends signals to the hypothalamus, which triggers the release of stress hormones like adrenaline and cortisol.

- Physical Reactions: These hormones prepare the body for action by increasing heart rate, blood pressure, and respiration. Blood flow is redirected from the internal organs to the muscles, preparing the body to either confront the threat or flee from it. This is why people often experience physical symptoms like a racing heart, tense muscles, and rapid breathing when they are angry.

- The Role of the Autonomic Nervous System: The autonomic nervous system (ANS) is responsible for regulating involuntary body functions, including those associated with anger. The ANS is divided into two branches: the sympathetic nervous system (SNS) and the parasympathetic nervous system (PNS). The SNS is responsible for the body's fight-or-flight response, while the PNS helps calm the body down after the perceived threat has passed.

When anger is triggered, the SNS dominates, leading to the physiological changes mentioned earlier. However, chronic or intense anger can overwhelm the body's ability to return to a calm state, leading to prolonged stress and potential health issues, such as hypertension, heart disease, and weakened immune function.

Psychological Aspects of Anger

Anger is also deeply intertwined with our psychological processes. It is influenced by our thoughts, beliefs, and perceptions, making it a highly individualized experience. Understanding the psychological aspects of anger requires us to examine the cognitive processes that contribute to its emergence and how these processes can be managed or altered.

- Cognitive Appraisal: One of the key psychological components of anger is cognitive appraisal, which refers to the way we interpret and evaluate situations. When we perceive an event as threatening, unjust, or frustrating, our cognitive appraisal can trigger anger. For example, if a parent perceives a child's disobedience as a challenge to their authority, they may become angry. However, if the same behavior is interpreted as a sign of the child's independence, the emotional response might be different.

- Beliefs and Expectations: Our beliefs and expectations play a significant role in how we experience anger. Unmet expectations, such as expecting others to behave in a certain way or anticipating specific outcomes, can lead to feelings of frustration and anger. For instance, a parent who believes that children should always be obedient may become easily angered when their child does not conform to this expectation.

- Emotional Regulation: Emotional regulation refers to our ability to manage and respond to emotional experiences in a healthy and adaptive way. Some people have a natural ability to regulate their emotions effectively, while others may struggle with this skill. Poor emotional regulation can lead to heightened and prolonged anger, making it difficult to respond to situations calmly and rationally.

- Personality Traits: Certain personality traits can make individuals more prone to anger. For example, individuals with a high level of neuroticism or those who are easily frustrated may be more likely to experience anger. Conversely, people with a more easy-going or resilient temperament may be less prone to anger.

The Role of Anger in Human Behavior

Anger is a driving force in human behavior, influencing our actions, decisions, and interactions with others. While it is often viewed as a negative emotion, anger can also have positive functions, depending on how it is expressed and managed.

- Motivation for Change: Anger can serve as a powerful motivator for change. When channeled constructively, it can lead to actions that address injustices, resolve conflicts, and improve situations. For example, a parent who becomes angry about a child's dangerous behavior might use that anger to enforce stricter safety rules, ultimately protecting the child.

- Expression of Boundaries: Anger can be a way of expressing personal boundaries and asserting one's rights. It can signal to others that certain behaviors are unacceptable and that changes are needed. For instance, a parent might become angry when their child repeatedly disrespects household rules, prompting a discussion about the importance of respect and cooperation.

- Communication and Conflict Resolution: Anger, when expressed appropriately, can be a tool for communication and conflict resolution. It can bring underlying issues to the surface, allowing for open discussion and problem-solving. However, it is crucial that anger is expressed in a controlled and constructive manner to prevent escalation and harm.

- Negative Consequences: While anger can have positive effects, it also carries significant risks when not managed properly. Uncontrolled anger can lead to aggressive behavior, strained relationships, and even violence. In the context of parenting, frequent and intense anger can create a hostile home environment, damaging the parent-child relationship and hindering a child's emotional development.

Understanding the definition and nature of anger is the first step in learning how to manage it effectively. By recognizing that anger is both a physiological and psychological response, we can begin to explore the underlying factors that trigger it and develop strategies for controlling it. Anger is a natural and necessary emotion, but it must be managed with care and awareness, especially in the context of parenting, where its impact can have lasting effects on both the parent and the child.

In the following chapters, we will delve deeper into the various strategies and techniques that can be used to manage anger, drawing on insights from philosophy, psychology, and theology. By integrating these perspectives, we aim to provide a comprehensive approach to anger management that is both practical and meaningful for parents.

Philosophical Perspective on Anger

Anger has been a subject of deep contemplation and debate throughout the history of philosophy. Philosophers, both ancient and modern, have sought to understand the nature of anger, its causes, and its consequences, as well as to prescribe methods for managing it. Among the most influential philosophical perspectives on anger are those of Aristotle and the Stoics, each offering distinct but complementary approaches to understanding and moderating this powerful emotion.

Aristotle's Perspective on Anger and Temperance

Aristotle, one of the most renowned philosophers of ancient Greece, devoted considerable attention to the study of emotions in his ethical writings, particularly in his work Nicomachean Ethics. Aristotle did not view anger as inherently bad; instead, he believed that anger, like other emotions, should be expressed in a balanced and measured way, a concept he described through the virtue of temperance.

The Doctrine of the Mean

Central to Aristotle's ethical thought is the Doctrine of the Mean, which posits that virtue lies in finding the balance between excess and deficiency. In the case of anger, Aristotle argued that the virtuous individual is one who experiences anger to the right degree, at the right time, for the right reasons, and towards the right people. This balanced expression of anger is what Aristotle referred to as "righteous indignation."

According to Aristotle, there are two extremes of anger that should be avoided:

- Irascibility (Excessive Anger): This is the condition of being too easily angered or prone to excessive displays of anger. Irascible individuals may react violently or disproportionately to minor provocations, leading to destructive consequences for themselves and others.

- Apathy (Deficiency of Anger): On the other end of the spectrum is apathy, the lack of appropriate anger when it is warranted. Aristotle considered this equally problematic, as it could result in passivity in the face of injustice or wrongdoing.

Righteous Indignation

Aristotle's ideal is the person who feels "righteous indignation," a controlled and appropriate response to wrongdoing. This person is neither excessively angry nor indifferent; they recognize when anger is justified and express it in a way that is constructive rather than destructive.

For Aristotle, the key to managing anger lies in the development of temperance, a virtue that allows individuals to control their impulses and respond to situations with reasoned judgment rather than raw emotion. In the context of parenting, this means cultivating the ability to respond to a child's misbehavior with measured and thoughtful anger, rather than reacting impulsively.

The Role of Reason in Anger

Aristotle also emphasized the role of reason in managing anger. He believed that anger, when properly guided by reason, could be a force for justice and moral action. However, when divorced from reason, anger could lead to rash and harmful decisions. Thus, Aristotle encouraged the cultivation of reason and self-discipline as essential components of virtuous living, including in the management of anger.

In summary, Aristotle's approach to anger management is grounded in the idea of balance and moderation. By cultivating temperance and allowing reason to guide emotional responses, individuals can express anger in ways that are just, appropriate, and ultimately beneficial.

Stoic Philosophy and the Control of Anger

While Aristotle advocated for a balanced expression of anger, the Stoics took a more radical stance, arguing that anger should be entirely eradicated. The Stoic school of philosophy, founded by Zeno of Citium in the early 3rd century BCE, emphasized the importance of living in accordance with nature and reason, and viewed anger as a destructive and irrational emotion that should be avoided at all costs.

The Stoic View on Emotions

The Stoics believed that emotions like anger arise from false judgments and a lack of rational control. According to Stoic philosophy, external events are neither inherently good nor bad; it is our interpretations of these events that lead to emotional responses. Anger, therefore, is the result of an erroneous belief that something outside of our control has wronged us and that this wrong justifies an emotional reaction.

The Stoic approach to managing anger involves changing our perceptions and judgments about the events that trigger it. By recognizing that we cannot control external circumstances, but only our responses to them, we can free ourselves from the grip of anger.

Seneca on Anger

One of the most famous Stoic philosophers, Seneca, wrote extensively on the subject of anger in his work De Ira (On Anger). Seneca argued that anger is not only irrational but also dangerous, leading to destructive behaviors and harmful consequences. He believed that anger distorts reason, making it impossible to think clearly and act justly.

Seneca advised several practical strategies for avoiding anger:

- Anticipation: By anticipating potential provocations and preparing for them mentally, individuals can reduce the likelihood of becoming angry when these events occur.

- Delay: Seneca recommended delaying any response when anger begins to rise. By postponing action, individuals can give themselves time to calm down and respond more rationally.

- Perspective: The Stoics emphasized the importance of perspective, reminding themselves that many things that provoke anger are trivial or insignificant in the grand scheme of life. By focusing on what is truly important, individuals can avoid getting caught up in minor irritations.

Epictetus and the Control of Emotions

Epictetus, another prominent Stoic philosopher, echoed similar ideas in his teachings. He emphasized the importance of understanding what is within our control and what is not. According to Epictetus, our emotions are within our control because they are the result of our judgments. By adjusting our judgments, we can change our emotional responses.

Epictetus famously taught that it is not events themselves that disturb us, but our interpretations of them. This teaching has profound implications for anger management. If we can change the way we interpret and respond to provocations, we can prevent anger from arising in the first place.

The Stoic Ideal: Apatheia

The ultimate goal for the Stoics was to achieve apatheia, a state of being free from irrational emotions, including anger. This does not mean being emotionless but rather maintaining a sense of inner peace and rational control, regardless of external circumstances. For the Stoics, the eradication of anger was a key aspect of living a virtuous and rational life.

In the context of parenting, the Stoic approach suggests that parents should strive to maintain calmness and rationality in all situations, recognizing that anger is not a necessary or helpful response to their child's behavior. By practicing Stoic principles, parents can learn to manage their emotional responses and create a more peaceful and harmonious family environment.

Modern Philosophical Views on Anger

While ancient philosophers like Aristotle and the Stoics laid the groundwork for understanding and managing anger, modern philosophy has continued to explore these themes, often integrating insights from psychology and other disciplines.

Existentialist Perspectives

Existentialist philosophers, such as Jean-Paul Sartre and Albert Camus, have examined anger through the lens of individual freedom and responsibility. Existentialists argue that anger often arises from a sense of frustration with the constraints of existence or the perceived absurdity of life. In this view, anger is a response to the tension between our desire for control and the reality of our limited power.

Existentialist philosophy suggests that by embracing our freedom and taking responsibility for our choices, we can mitigate the anger that arises from feelings of powerlessness or injustice. This approach emphasizes the importance of self-awareness and personal agency in managing anger.

Contemporary Ethical Theories

Contemporary ethical theories, such as those rooted in virtue ethics or deontological ethics, continue to explore the role of anger in moral behavior. Some modern philosophers argue that anger can be a justifiable and even necessary response to moral wrongs, particularly when it motivates individuals to act against injustice.

However, these theories also stress the importance of ensuring that anger is proportionate, justified, and directed toward constructive ends. In this sense, modern philosophy often echoes Aristotle's emphasis on temperance and the balanced expression of anger.

Philosophy and Anger Management Today

In today's world, philosophical perspectives on anger are increasingly integrated with psychological approaches to provide a comprehensive framework for anger management.

By drawing on the wisdom of both ancient and modern philosophers, individuals can develop a deeper understanding of anger and learn to manage it in ways that promote personal growth, healthy relationships, and social harmony.

Philosophy offers a rich and nuanced understanding of anger, providing valuable insights into how this powerful emotion can be managed and directed. Aristotle's emphasis on temperance and the balanced expression of anger, combined with the Stoic focus on rational control and the eradication of destructive emotions, provides a robust foundation for anger management.

For parents, these philosophical perspectives offer practical tools and guiding principles for managing anger in a way that is both constructive and virtuous. By cultivating temperance, practicing reasoned judgment, and striving for inner peace, parents can learn to manage their anger effectively, creating a more positive and supportive environment for their children.

In the next chapter, we will explore the psychological aspects of anger, examining how cognitive-behavioral techniques and emotional regulation strategies can be used to manage anger in everyday parenting situations. By combining these philosophical insights with psychological tools, we can develop a comprehensive approach to anger management that is both practical and deeply meaningful.

New Testament Teachings

In the New Testament, the teachings of Jesus and the apostles further develop the Biblical understanding of anger, emphasizing love, forgiveness, and reconciliation as central tenets of Christian life. The Sermon on the Mount, one of Jesus' most significant discourses, addresses the issue of anger directly:

- Matthew 5:21-22: "You have heard that it was said to the people long ago, 'You shall not murder, and anyone who murders will be subject to judgment.' But I tell you that anyone who is angry with a brother or sister will be subject to judgment. Again, anyone who says to a brother or sister, 'Raca,' is answerable to the court. And anyone who says, 'You fool!' will be in danger of the fire of hell."

In this passage, Jesus expands the scope of moral responsibility beyond outward actions like murder to include internal emotions such as anger. He teaches that harboring anger and expressing it in harmful ways is spiritually dangerous and leads to judgment. This highlights the importance of addressing anger not just in behavior, but in the heart and mind.

The apostle Paul also addresses anger in his epistles, offering practical guidance for Christian living:

- Ephesians 4:26-27: "In your anger do not sin: Do not let the sun go down while you are still angry, and do not give the devil a foothold."

- Colossians 3:8: "But now you must also rid yourselves of all such things as these: anger, rage, malice, slander, and filthy language from your lips."

Paul acknowledges that anger is a natural human emotion but emphasizes the importance of not allowing it to lead to sin. The instruction to "not let the sun go down" on anger suggests the need for timely resolution and reconciliation, preventing anger from festering and leading to further conflict.

Righteous Anger and the Example of Jesus

The New Testament also presents the concept of righteous anger through the example of Jesus. One of the most well-known instances of Jesus expressing anger is when He drives the money changers out of the temple:

- John 2:13-16: "When it was almost time for the Jewish Passover, Jesus went up to Jerusalem. In the temple courts he found people selling cattle, sheep and doves, and others sitting at tables exchanging money. So he made a whip out of cords, and drove all from the temple courts, both sheep and cattle; he scattered the coins of the money changers and overturned their tables. To those who sold doves he said, 'Get these out of here! Stop turning my Father's house into a market!'"

In this passage, Jesus' anger is directed at the desecration of the temple, which was intended to be a house of prayer. His actions are motivated by zeal for God's honor and the desire to restore the sanctity of the temple. This episode illustrates that anger, when rooted in righteousness and aligned with divine principles, can be an appropriate response to injustice and wrongdoing.

However, the broader message of the New Testament is one of love and forgiveness, encouraging believers to seek peace and avoid unnecessary conflict. The teachings of Jesus and the apostles call Christians to transcend anger through the practice of compassion, patience, and forgiveness.

Anger in Judaism

Judaism shares many similarities with Christianity regarding the understanding of anger, as both traditions are rooted in the Hebrew Scriptures. In Jewish thought, anger is recognized as a natural emotion that must be controlled and directed toward constructive purposes.

The Talmudic Perspective

The Talmud, a central text in Rabbinic Judaism, contains numerous teachings on anger. It often advises against succumbing to anger, emphasizing the importance of self-control and humility. The Talmud warns that anger can lead to destructive consequences and can distance a person from God.

For example, in Pirkei Avot (Ethics of the Fathers), a collection of ethical teachings from the Mishnah, it is said:

- "Who is strong? One who subdues his inclination" (Pirkei Avot 4:1).

This teaching reflects the Jewish emphasis on mastering one's emotions and inclinations, including anger, as a sign of true strength and spiritual maturity.

Kabbalistic Interpretations

Kabbalistic teachings, which explore the mystical aspects of Judaism, also address the concept of anger. In Kabbalah, anger is seen as a force that can disrupt the spiritual harmony of the individual and the world. The Kabbalists teach that anger arises from the ego and the illusion of separation from the divine. By recognizing the divine presence in all things and cultivating humility, one can transcend anger and attain inner peace.

Anger in Islam

Islamic teachings also address anger, recognizing it as a natural human emotion that must be managed according to the principles of faith. The Qur'an and Hadith (sayings and actions of the Prophet Muhammad) provide guidance on how Muslims should approach and control anger.

Qur'anic Teachings

The Qur'an emphasizes patience and forgiveness as virtues that help believers manage their anger:

- Surah Al-Imran 3:134: "Those who spend [in Allah's cause] in prosperity and in adversity, who repress anger, and who pardon men; verily, Allah loves the good-doers."

This verse highlights the importance of repressing anger and extending forgiveness, which are seen as qualities that are beloved by God. The Qur'an encourages believers to exercise self-restraint and to seek forgiveness from God as a way of overcoming anger.

Hadith on Anger Management

The Hadith literature offers practical advice on controlling anger. The Prophet Muhammad is reported to have said:

- "The strong is not the one who overcomes the people by his strength, but the strong is the one who controls himself while in anger." (Sahih al-Bukhari)

This Hadith emphasizes that true strength lies in self-control rather than physical prowess. The Prophet Muhammad also advised practical measures to calm anger, such as sitting down, lying down, performing ablution (wudu), and seeking refuge in God from the Devil.

In Islam, anger is viewed as a test of character. By managing anger and choosing patience and forgiveness,

Muslims can demonstrate their faith and align their actions with divine will.

Anger in Buddhism

Buddhism offers a unique perspective on anger, viewing it as one of the "Three Poisons" that hinder spiritual development. The other two poisons are greed and ignorance. In Buddhist teachings, anger is considered a destructive emotion that leads to suffering for oneself and others.

The Four Noble Truths and Anger

Central to Buddhist thought are the Four Noble Truths, which outline the nature of suffering and the path to its cessation. Anger is seen as a manifestation of suffering (dukkha) and as a cause of further suffering.

- First Noble Truth: Life contains suffering.

- Second Noble Truth: The cause of suffering is attachment, aversion, and ignorance.

- Third Noble Truth: There is a way to end suffering.

- Fourth Noble Truth: The path to ending suffering is the Noble Eightfold Path.

The second truth identifies aversion, which includes anger, as a root cause of suffering. Therefore, one of the key goals in Buddhism is to overcome anger through mindfulness, compassion, and the cultivation of inner peace.

Meditation and Mindfulness

Buddhist practices such as meditation and mindfulness are central to managing anger. Mindfulness helps individuals become aware of their anger as it arises, allowing them to observe it without being consumed by it. Meditation practices, particularly loving-kindness meditation (Metta Bhavana), are designed to cultivate compassion and reduce anger.

Through these practices, Buddhists learn to transform anger into compassion and understanding, ultimately leading to a state of equanimity and peace.

Anger in Hinduism

Hinduism, with its diverse philosophical and spiritual traditions, also addresses anger as an emotion that must be controlled to achieve spiritual growth. The Bhagavad Gita, one of Hinduism's most important scriptures, provides guidance on managing anger within the context of duty and righteousness (dharma).

The Bhagavad Gita and Anger

In the Bhagavad Gita, Lord Krishna advises the warrior Arjuna on the importance of self-control and detachment from the fruits of action. Anger is described as one of the obstacles to spiritual progress:

- Bhagavad Gita 2:63: "From anger comes delusion; from delusion, bewilderment of memory; when memory is bewildered, intelligence is lost, and when intelligence is lost, one falls down again into the material pool."

This verse outlines the negative consequences of anger, which lead to a loss of clarity and wisdom. Krishna advises Arjuna to maintain a balanced mind, free from attachment and aversion, as the path to liberation (moksha).

The Concept of Ahimsa

Ahimsa, or non-violence, is a fundamental principle in Hinduism that extends to thoughts and emotions. Practicing ahimsa involves cultivating an attitude of non-violence toward all living beings, including oneself. This principle encourages individuals to manage anger and other harmful emotions by fostering love, compassion, and forgiveness.

Through the practice of yoga, meditation, and devotion (bhakti), Hindus seek to purify their minds and hearts, overcoming anger and achieving a state of inner peace and harmony.

Religious teachings from various faith traditions offer profound insights into the nature of anger and how it can be managed in accordance with spiritual principles. Whether through the wisdom of the Bible, the teachings of the Qur'an, the meditative practices of Buddhism, or the spiritual guidance of the Bhagavad Gita, these traditions emphasize the importance of self-control, patience, and compassion in overcoming anger.

For parents, these teachings provide valuable guidance for managing anger in a way that aligns with their faith and promotes a peaceful and loving family environment. By drawing on the wisdom of their religious traditions, parents can learn to respond to anger with grace and understanding, fostering healthier relationships and setting a positive example for their children.

In the following chapters, we will explore psychological strategies and practical tools for anger management, integrating these theological insights into a comprehensive approach that addresses both the spiritual and emotional dimensions of anger.

CHAPTER 02

THE PSYCHOLOGY OF ANGER

Anger is not only a fundamental human emotion but also a complex psychological phenomenon that has been the subject of extensive study. Various psychological theories have sought to explain the origins, triggers, and consequences of anger, as well as to provide strategies for managing it effectively. In this chapter, we will explore key psychological theories related to anger, focusing on cognitive-behavioral theories and emotional regulation.

Cognitive-Behavioral Theories of Anger

Cognitive-behavioral theories (CBT) are among the most influential in understanding and managing anger. These theories emphasize the role of thoughts (cognitions) and behaviors in shaping emotional responses, including anger. CBT posits that anger is often the result of distorted or maladaptive thinking patterns, which lead to negative emotions and behaviors.

1. The Cognitive Model of Anger

The cognitive model of anger suggests that the way individuals interpret and perceive events plays a crucial role in whether they experience anger. According to this model, anger arises from the interaction between a triggering event, the individual's interpretation of that event, and the resulting emotional response.

- Triggering Event: This could be any external stimulus that the individual perceives as a threat, frustration, or injustice. For example, a parent might feel angered when their child disobeys a rule.

- Cognitive Appraisal: The individual's interpretation or appraisal of the event is critical. If the parent interprets the child's disobedience as a deliberate act of disrespect, they are more likely to experience anger. However, if they view it as a misunderstanding or a developmental stage, the emotional response might be less intense.

- Emotional Response: The cognitive appraisal leads to the emotional response—in this case, anger. The intensity and duration of the anger depend on the severity of the perceived threat or injustice and the individual's coping mechanisms.

2. Common Cognitive Distortions Leading to Anger

Cognitive-behavioral theorists have identified several common cognitive distortions that contribute to anger:

- Catastrophizing: This involves imagining the worst possible outcome of a situation, leading to heightened feelings of anger and anxiety. For example, a parent might catastrophize by believing that their child's disobedience is a sign that they are losing control as a parent.

- Overgeneralization: This occurs when a person takes a single negative event and generalizes it to all situations. A parent might overgeneralize by thinking, "My child never listens to me," based on a single incident.

- Personalization: This distortion involves taking things personally and blaming oneself for events outside one's control. A parent might personalize their child's behavior, interpreting it as a reflection of their failure as a parent.

- Mind Reading: Assuming that others are deliberately trying to provoke or harm us without evidence. A parent might believe that their child is intentionally trying to make them angry, even if that is not the case.

3. Cognitive Restructuring

One of the core strategies in cognitive-behavioral therapy for managing anger is cognitive restructuring. This process involves identifying and challenging cognitive distortions and replacing them with more rational and balanced thoughts. By changing the way one thinks about a situation, it is possible to alter the emotional response and reduce anger.

For example, a parent who initially thinks, "My child is deliberately trying to defy me" might use cognitive restructuring to change their thought to, "My child is acting out because they are frustrated and don't know how to express it." This shift in perspective can lead to a more compassionate and measured response, reducing the likelihood of anger.

Emotional Regulation and Anger

Emotional regulation refers to the processes by which individuals influence the emotions they experience, when they experience them, and how they express them. Effective emotional regulation is essential for managing anger, as it helps individuals maintain control over their emotional responses and avoid destructive behavior.

1. Theories of Emotional Regulation

Several theories have been proposed to explain how people regulate their emotions, with two of the most prominent being the process model of emotion regulation and the dual-process model.

- Process Model of Emotion Regulation: Developed by James Gross, this model outlines the different stages at which emotion regulation can occur, from the selection of situations to the modulation of emotional responses. The five key stages are:

- Situation Selection: Choosing environments or situations that are less likely to trigger anger. For example, a parent might avoid discussing contentious topics with their child when they are already feeling stressed.

- Situation Modification: Altering a situation to make it less likely to provoke anger. A parent might modify a situation by setting clear expectations for behavior before entering a potentially challenging situation.

- Attention Deployment: Redirecting attention away from anger-provoking stimuli. A parent might focus on their child's positive qualities rather than their frustrating behavior.

- Cognitive Change: Reappraising the situation to alter its emotional impact, similar to cognitive restructuring. A parent might reinterpret a child's tantrum as a sign of needing comfort rather than defiance.

- Response Modulation: Modulating the emotional response after it has been generated, such as using relaxation techniques to calm down after becoming angry.

- Dual-Process Model: This model suggests that emotional regulation involves both automatic and controlled processes. Automatic processes are quick, unconscious responses to emotional stimuli, while controlled processes involve deliberate efforts to regulate emotions. Effective anger management often requires shifting from automatic, reactive responses to more controlled, deliberate strategies.

2. Strategies for Emotional Regulation

There are several practical strategies for emotional regulation that can help manage anger:

- Mindfulness: Mindfulness involves paying attention to the present moment without judgment. Practicing mindfulness can help individuals become more aware of their anger as it arises, allowing them to respond more calmly and thoughtfully.

- Breathing Exercises: Deep breathing exercises can help regulate the body's physiological response to anger, such as increased heart rate and tension. By focusing on slow, deep breaths, individuals can activate the parasympathetic nervous system, which promotes relaxation and reduces the intensity of anger.

Progressive Muscle Relaxation: This technique involves tensing and then slowly relaxing each muscle group in the body. Progressive muscle relaxation can help reduce the physical tension associated with anger, making it easier to manage the emotional response.

- Delay and Distraction: Delaying a response to anger by taking a break or distracting oneself can prevent immediate, impulsive reactions. This delay provides time for the individual to cool down and think more clearly before responding.

- Expressive Writing: Writing about feelings of anger can be a cathartic way to process emotions. By putting thoughts and feelings into words, individuals can gain clarity and perspective, reducing the intensity of their anger.

3. Emotional Intelligence and Anger Management

Emotional intelligence (EI) is the ability to recognize, understand, and manage one's own emotions, as well as the emotions of others. High emotional intelligence is associated with better anger management, as it involves skills such as self-awareness, empathy, and effective communication.

- Self-Awareness: Being aware of one's emotional triggers and responses is the first step in managing anger. Self-awareness allows individuals to recognize when they are becoming angry and to take proactive steps to manage it.

- Empathy: Understanding and empathizing with others' perspectives can reduce anger by fostering compassion and reducing the tendency to blame. For example, a parent who empathizes with their child's frustration is less likely to react with anger.

- Communication Skills: Effective communication involves expressing emotions in a clear, respectful, and non-confrontational manner. Assertive communication can help resolve conflicts without escalating anger, leading to more positive outcomes in relationships.

Anger as a Learned Behavior

Another important aspect of psychological theories on anger is the concept of anger as a learned behavior. Social learning theory, developed by Albert Bandura, suggests that individuals learn behaviors, including anger, through observation and imitation of others.

1. Modeling and Imitation

Children often learn how to express anger by observing their parents and other significant figures in their lives. If a child frequently witnesses aggressive or uncontrolled expressions of anger, they may learn to imitate these behaviors. Conversely, if a child observes calm and constructive ways of dealing with anger, they are more likely to adopt these behaviors themselves.

2. Reinforcement and Punishment

The expression of anger can also be reinforced or punished by the reactions of others. For example, if a child learns that throwing a tantrum results in getting what they want, this behavior is reinforced and is more likely to occur in the future. On the other hand, if calm and respectful communication is rewarded, the child is more likely to adopt this approach.

Understanding anger as a learned behavior highlights the importance of modeling appropriate anger management strategies for children. Parents play a crucial role in teaching their children how to handle anger by demonstrating constructive and effective ways of dealing with frustration and conflict.

The psychological theories discussed in this chapter provide a comprehensive framework for understanding anger and developing strategies to manage it. Cognitive-behavioral theories emphasize the importance of recognizing and challenging distorted thinking patterns that lead to anger, while emotional regulation theories offer practical tools for managing the emotional response itself.

By integrating these psychological insights into daily life, individuals can learn to control their anger more effectively, leading to healthier relationships and improved emotional well-being. For parents, these strategies are particularly valuable, as they not only help manage their own anger but also serve as a model for their children, teaching them how to navigate their emotions in a healthy and constructive way.

In the next chapter, we will explore the practical application of these psychological strategies in everyday parenting situations, providing tools and exercises to help parents manage anger and create a more peaceful family environment.

Anger Triggers in Parenting

Parenting is a complex and emotionally demanding role, and it is natural for parents to experience anger at times. Understanding the common triggers that provoke anger in parenting is crucial for managing this emotion effectively. By identifying these triggers, parents can better anticipate and address situations that may lead to anger, ultimately fostering healthier relationships and more positive interactions with their children. In this chapter, we will explore some of the most common anger triggers in parenting and examine how they affect behavior and relationships within the family.

Common Anger Triggers in Parenting

1. Disobedience and Defiance

One of the most common triggers for parental anger is a child's disobedience or defiance. When children do not follow rules or directly challenge authority, it can lead to frustration and anger in parents. This response is often tied to a parent's desire to maintain order, discipline, and respect within the household.

- Impact on Behavior: When parents react to disobedience or defiance with anger, it can lead to escalating conflicts. The child may respond with further defiance, leading to a cycle of confrontation. Over time, this can strain the parent-child relationship and create a hostile environment in the home.

- Impact on Relationships: Consistent anger in response to defiance can damage trust and communication between parents and children. Children may begin to associate parental authority with fear and punishment rather than guidance and support, which can hinder their emotional development and lead to resentment.

2. Tantrums and Emotional Outbursts

Young children, in particular, are prone to tantrums and emotional outbursts, which can be highly triggering for parents. These episodes often occur when a child is unable to express their needs or emotions effectively, leading to frustration for both the child and the parent.

- Impact on Behavior: Parental anger in response to tantrums can exacerbate the situation. Instead of calming the child, the parent's anger may increase the child's distress, making it more difficult to resolve the situation. This can also reinforce the child's use of tantrums as a way to gain attention or control.

- Impact on Relationships: Frequent angry responses to tantrums can weaken the parent-child bond. Children may feel misunderstood or unsupported, leading to feelings of insecurity. Additionally, parents may feel guilty or ashamed after reacting in anger, which can affect their confidence in their parenting abilities.

3. Sibling Rivalry and Conflicts

Sibling rivalry and conflicts are another common trigger for parental anger. When children argue, fight, or compete for attention, it can create tension and frustration for parents, who may struggle to mediate these conflicts effectively.

- Impact on Behavior: Parental anger in response to sibling rivalry can lead to biased or unfair treatment, where one child is perceived as the "problem" and the other as the "victim." This can increase animosity between siblings and lead to feelings of favoritism or resentment.

- Impact on Relationships: Ongoing anger in response to sibling conflicts can create a toxic family dynamic. Siblings may feel that they are constantly in competition for their parents' approval, leading to long-term relationship issues. Moreover, parents may feel overwhelmed and powerless to create harmony in the household.

4. Disrespectful Behavior

Disrespectful behavior, such as talking back, ignoring requests, or showing a lack of gratitude, is another significant trigger for parental anger. Parents often expect a certain level of respect and cooperation from their children, and when these expectations are not met, it can lead to feelings of frustration and anger.

- Impact on Behavior: Responding to disrespect with anger can escalate the situation, leading to more confrontational interactions. The child may become defensive or even more disrespectful, reinforcing the negative behavior.

- Impact on Relationships: Persistent anger in response to perceived disrespect can erode the mutual respect and understanding that are essential for a healthy parent-child relationship. Children may feel alienated or misunderstood, while parents may feel disrespected and undervalued.

5. Lack of Cooperation and Responsibility

Parents often become angry when their children fail to cooperate or take responsibility for their actions, such as not completing chores, neglecting schoolwork, or failing to follow through on commitments. This can be particularly frustrating for parents who value discipline and responsibility.

- Impact on Behavior: Anger in response to a lack of cooperation can lead to a breakdown in communication and an increase in power struggles. Children may become more resistant to following instructions or fulfilling their responsibilities, leading to further conflict.

Impact on Relationships: Over time, anger related to a lack of cooperation can create a punitive atmosphere in the home. Children may feel pressured or coerced, rather than motivated by a sense of responsibility or mutual respect. This can lead to feelings of resentment and a lack of intrinsic motivation.

6. Parenting Stress and Overwhelm

Parenting is inherently stressful, and the demands of managing a household, work, and childcare can be overwhelming. When parents are already stressed or overwhelmed, they are more likely to react with anger to everyday challenges.

- Impact on Behavior: Stress-induced anger can lead to impulsive or disproportionate reactions to minor infractions. Parents may find themselves yelling or punishing their children for behaviors that they would normally address more calmly.

- Impact on Relationships: Chronic stress and anger can create a tense and negative home environment, where both parents and children feel on edge. This can lead to a breakdown in communication, increased conflict, and a general sense of dissatisfaction within the family.

7. Unrealistic Expectations

Parents sometimes hold unrealistic expectations for their children's behavior, maturity, or abilities. When children fail to meet these expectations, it can trigger anger and disappointment.

- Impact on Behavior: Holding children to unrealistic standards can lead to frequent criticism and punishment, which can damage their self-esteem and discourage them from trying to meet expectations in the future.

- Impact on Relationships: Unrealistic expectations and the anger they provoke can create a sense of inadequacy in children. They may feel that they can never satisfy their parents, leading to feelings of frustration and hopelessness. This can strain the parent-child relationship and lead to long-term emotional issues.

8. External Pressures and Comparisons

Parents may also experience anger when they feel pressured by external factors, such as societal expectations, comparisons with other families, or the desire for their children to succeed academically or socially. These pressures can lead to anger when parents perceive that their children are not living up to these standards.

- Impact on Behavior: External pressures can lead to a hyper-focus on performance and success, causing parents to react angrily when their children fall short. This can create a stressful and competitive environment, where children feel constantly judged.

- Impact on Relationships: Comparing children to others and reacting with anger when they do not measure up can damage their self-worth and the parent-child relationship. Children may feel that they are valued only for their achievements, rather than for who they are as individuals.

9. Personal Insecurities and Unresolved Issues

Parents' own insecurities and unresolved emotional issues can be a significant trigger for anger. For example, a parent who struggled with authority as a child may feel especially triggered when their child challenges their authority.

- Impact on Behavior: When anger is rooted in personal insecurities, it can lead to irrational or exaggerated reactions. Parents may project their unresolved issues onto their children, leading to unfair or overly harsh treatment.

- Impact on Relationships: Anger stemming from personal insecurities can create a disconnect between parents and children. Children may feel confused by the intensity of their parents' reactions and struggle to understand why their behavior elicits such strong emotions.

10. Fatigue and Sleep Deprivation

Fatigue and sleep deprivation are common among parents, especially those with young children. When parents are tired, their tolerance for frustration is significantly reduced, making them more prone to anger.

- Impact on Behavior: Sleep-deprived parents may find themselves snapping at their children or losing their temper more easily. This can lead to a cycle of guilt and frustration, as parents struggle to maintain control over their emotions.

- Impact on Relationships: Chronic fatigue and the resulting anger can create a sense of distance and disconnection between parents and children. Children may feel that their parents are constantly irritable or unavailable, leading to feelings of neglect or rejection.

The Ripple Effect: How Anger Affects Behavior and Relationships

Understanding the triggers of anger in parenting is only the first step. It is equally important to recognize how anger affects behavior and relationships within the family. When parents react to these triggers with anger, it can have both immediate and long-term consequences for their children and the overall family dynamic.

1. Modeling Behavior

Children learn how to manage their emotions by observing their parents. When parents consistently respond to challenges with anger, children are likely to mimic this behavior. They may learn to view anger as an acceptable or even necessary response to frustration, leading to difficulties in managing their own emotions.

2. Escalating Conflicts

Anger often leads to escalating conflicts within the family. What might begin as a minor disagreement can quickly turn into a full-blown argument when anger is involved. This can create a cycle of conflict, where both parents and children become increasingly defensive and combative.

3. Impact on Emotional Development

Frequent exposure to parental anger can have a significant impact on a child's emotional development. Children may develop anxiety, fear, or low self-esteem as a result of their parents' anger. They may also struggle with emotional regulation, leading to difficulties in forming healthy relationships later in life.

4. Erosion of Trust

Trust is a fundamental component of any healthy relationship, including the parent-child relationship. When anger is a frequent presence in the home, it can erode trust between parents and children. Children may feel that they cannot rely on their parents for support or understanding, leading to a breakdown in communication and connection.

5. Long-Term Relationship Strain

Over time, unresolved anger and the conflicts it causes can strain the parent-child relationship. Children who grow up in an environment where anger is prevalent may become distant, resentful, or rebellious. This can lead to long-term challenges in maintaining a positive and supportive relationship as they grow older.

Anger triggers in parenting are varied and complex, but understanding them is crucial for managing this powerful emotion effectively. By recognizing the situations and behaviors that provoke anger, parents can take proactive steps to address these triggers and reduce the likelihood of negative outcomes.

In the following chapters, we will explore strategies for managing these anger triggers, drawing on psychological, philosophical, and theological insights. By learning to respond to anger triggers with patience, empathy, and self-control, parents can create a more peaceful and supportive environment for their children, fostering stronger and healthier relationships in the process.

Managing Emotions

Strategies for Recognizing and Addressing Underlying Emotions that Contribute to Anger

Anger often arises as a surface emotion, masking deeper, underlying feelings that may be more challenging to recognize or express. These emotions can include fear, frustration, sadness, or a sense of powerlessness. To manage anger effectively, it is essential to understand and address these underlying emotions. This chapter will explore strategies for recognizing and dealing with these root causes, helping parents develop healthier emotional responses.

Understanding the Role of Underlying Emotions

Anger rarely exists in isolation. It is typically a secondary emotion, triggered by other, more vulnerable feelings. For example, a parent may become angry when their child misbehaves, but the underlying emotion could be fear—fear that they are losing control, fear for their child's safety, or fear of being judged as an inadequate parent.

Recognizing these underlying emotions is crucial because it allows for a more accurate and compassionate understanding of one's emotional state. By addressing the root cause, rather than just the anger itself, parents can respond more effectively and reduce the frequency and intensity of their anger.

Common Underlying Emotions that Contribute to Anger

1. Fear

Fear is a powerful emotion that often underlies anger. It can stem from concerns about safety, the future, or the unknown. For parents, fear might arise from worries about their child's well-being, their own ability to parent effectively, or the potential consequences of their child's behavior.

- Example: A parent might react angrily when their child climbs onto a high ledge. While the immediate response is anger, the underlying emotion is likely fear—fear that the child might fall and get hurt.

2. Frustration

Frustration occurs when a goal is blocked or when things do not go as planned. In parenting, frustration can arise from daily challenges such as managing schedules, dealing with a child's refusal to cooperate, or struggling to balance multiple responsibilities.

- Example: A parent may feel angry when their child refuses to get ready for school on time. The underlying emotion is frustration, as the parent feels thwarted in their efforts to maintain order and stick to a schedule.

3. Sadness

Sadness or grief can also contribute to anger, especially when these emotions are not fully acknowledged or expressed. In parenting, sadness might be related to unmet expectations, the loss of personal freedom, or concerns about the child's future.

- Example: A parent might become angry when their child fails to meet academic expectations. Beneath the anger, there might be sadness about the child's struggles or disappointment over unmet hopes.

4. Powerlessness

Feelings of powerlessness or helplessness can lead to anger as a way to regain a sense of control. Parenting often involves situations where parents feel they have little control over outcomes, whether it's related to their child's behavior, external pressures, or life circumstances.

- Example: A parent might become angry when their child refuses to eat a healthy meal. The underlying emotion could be powerlessness, stemming from the parent's inability to ensure their child's well-being.

5. Guilt and Shame

Guilt and shame are emotions that can trigger anger, particularly when parents feel they have fallen short of their own or others' expectations. These emotions might be directed inward, but they can easily manifest as anger toward others, including children.

- Example: A parent might lash out in anger after making a mistake, such as forgetting an important school event. The underlying emotion is guilt for the oversight, which is redirected as anger toward the child or situation.

Strategies for Recognizing Underlying Emotions

1. Mindfulness and Self-Awareness

Mindfulness involves paying attention to the present moment without judgment. By practicing mindfulness, parents can become more aware of their emotional states as they arise, allowing them to identify the underlying emotions that contribute to anger.

- Practice: Take a few moments each day to sit quietly and observe your thoughts and feelings without trying to change them. Notice any sensations of tension, unease, or agitation, and explore what emotions might be beneath the surface.

- Application in Parenting: When you feel anger beginning to rise, pause and take a deep breath. Ask yourself, "What am I really feeling right now?" This can help you identify whether fear, frustration, sadness, or another emotion is driving your anger.

2. Emotional Labeling

Labeling emotions involves putting a name to what you are feeling. Research shows that simply labeling an emotion can reduce its intensity and make it easier to manage. By accurately labeling underlying emotions, parents can gain clarity and reduce the likelihood of reacting impulsively.

- Practice: When you notice yourself becoming angry, take a moment to label the emotion and any underlying feelings. For example, you might say to yourself, "I'm feeling frustrated because my child isn't listening," or "I'm feeling afraid that something bad might happen."

- Application in Parenting: Use emotional labeling with your children as well. For example, if your child is acting out, help them identify their emotions by saying, "It seems like you're feeling frustrated because you can't have what you want." This not only helps you understand their emotions but also teaches them emotional awareness.

3. Journaling

Journaling is a powerful tool for exploring emotions and gaining insight into your inner world. Writing about your experiences allows you to process emotions in a non-judgmental space, helping you uncover the underlying feelings that contribute to anger.

- Practice: Set aside time each day or week to write about your emotions. Reflect on moments when you felt angry and explore what might have been going on beneath the surface. What were you really feeling? What thoughts were driving those emotions?

- Application in Parenting: Consider keeping a "parenting journal" where you document challenging moments and your emotional responses. Over time, this can help you identify patterns and triggers, as well as recognize underlying emotions that need to be addressed.

4. Body Awareness

Emotions are not just mental experiences; they are also felt in the body. By paying attention to physical sensations, parents can gain clues about their emotional state and recognize underlying emotions before they escalate into anger.

- Practice: Regularly check in with your body throughout the day. Notice any areas of tension, discomfort, or tightness. These sensations can be indicators of underlying emotions that need attention.

- Application in Parenting: When you feel anger rising, do a quick body scan. Are your shoulders tense? Is your stomach in knots? Use these physical cues to identify the emotions you might be suppressing or ignoring.

5. Talking It Out

Sometimes, talking through your feelings with a trusted friend, partner, or therapist can help you gain clarity and insight. Verbalizing emotions allows you to process them more fully and can lead to the recognition of underlying emotions that contribute to anger.

- Practice: Find someone you trust and feel comfortable with to talk about your emotions. Discuss times when you felt angry and explore what might have been behind those feelings. Be open to feedback and different perspectives.

- Application in Parenting: If you have a co-parent, regularly discuss your parenting experiences and emotions together. Share moments when you felt angry and explore the underlying emotions with each other's support. This can strengthen your partnership and improve your emotional responses.

Strategies for Addressing Underlying Emotions

1. Developing Emotional Vocabulary

Building a rich emotional vocabulary allows you to express your feelings more accurately and effectively. When you can name and articulate your emotions, you are better equipped to address them in a healthy way.

- Practice: Expand your emotional vocabulary by learning and using a wide range of emotion words. Instead of simply saying "I'm angry," try to identify whether you are feeling "frustrated," "overwhelmed," "hurt," or "disappointed." This specificity can guide you toward appropriate solutions.

- Application in Parenting: Teach your children emotional vocabulary by using specific emotion words in your conversations. For example, instead of saying "You're mad," you might say, "It seems like you're feeling frustrated because your toy isn't working."

2. Addressing Root Causes

Once you have identified the underlying emotion, it's important to address its root cause. This might involve problem-solving, seeking support, or making changes in your environment or behavior.

- Practice: When you identify an underlying emotion like frustration or fear, ask yourself, "What is causing this feeling?" and "What can I do to address it?" If the emotion is frustration, for example, you might need to adjust your expectations or find more effective ways to communicate with your child.

- Application in Parenting: If you notice that certain situations consistently trigger underlying emotions, consider making changes to prevent those triggers. For instance, if mornings are stressful, you might establish a more organized routine to reduce frustration.

3. Self-Compassion

Self-compassion involves treating yourself with kindness and understanding when you are struggling with difficult emotions. By practicing self-compassion, you can create a supportive inner environment that allows you to address underlying emotions without self-judgment or criticism.

- Practice: When you recognize an underlying emotion, respond with self-compassion rather than self-criticism. For example, if you feel powerless, instead of berating yourself for not being in control, remind yourself that it's okay to feel this way and that you're doing your best.

- Application in Parenting: Model self-compassion for your children by being kind to yourself in front of them. When you make a mistake, acknowledge it without harsh self-judgment and demonstrate how you address your emotions constructively.

4. Creating Space for Emotions

It's important to create space for your emotions, allowing yourself time and room to process them fully. This might involve setting aside quiet time for reflection, engaging in activities that help you relax, or simply giving yourself permission to feel without the need to immediately "fix" things.

- Practice: Build time into your day for emotional reflection. This could be through meditation, taking a walk, or engaging in a hobby that allows you to process your feelings. Creating this space helps prevent emotions from building up and leading to anger.

- Application in Parenting: Encourage your children to create space for their emotions as well. Teach them that it's okay to take a break when they are feeling overwhelmed and that they can return to a problem with a clearer mind.

5. Seeking Professional Support

Sometimes, underlying emotions are deeply rooted or connected to past experiences that require professional support to address. Therapy or counseling can provide a safe space to explore these emotions and develop healthier ways to manage them.

- Practice: If you find that underlying emotions are consistently overwhelming or difficult to manage, consider seeking support from a therapist. Professional guidance can help you uncover and address deep-seated issues that contribute to anger.

- Application in Parenting: If you notice that your child is struggling with emotions that lead to anger, consider seeking professional support for them as well. A therapist can help your child develop emotional regulation skills and address any underlying issues.

Managing emotions, particularly the underlying feelings that contribute to anger, is a crucial skill for parents. By recognizing and addressing these emotions, parents can reduce the frequency and intensity of anger, leading to more constructive and compassionate responses to challenges.

The strategies outlined in this chapter—mindfulness, emotional labeling, journaling, body awareness, talking it out, developing emotional vocabulary, addressing root causes, practicing self-compassion, creating space for emotions, and seeking professional support—provide a comprehensive toolkit for managing emotions effectively. By integrating these practices into daily life, parents can enhance their emotional well-being and create a more supportive and nurturing environment for their children.

In the following chapters, we will explore how these strategies can be applied in specific parenting situations, helping you to navigate the challenges of parenthood with greater emotional resilience and understanding.

CHAPTER 03

PHILOSOPHICAL INSIGHTS INTO ANGER MANAGEMENT

Virtue Ethics: Cultivating Patience and Humility to Manage Anger

Anger, as a powerful and often disruptive emotion, has been the focus of philosophical inquiry for centuries. Among the many approaches to understanding and managing anger, virtue ethics stands out for its emphasis on character development and the cultivation of virtues that guide behavior. Virtue ethics, rooted in the teachings of ancient philosophers like Aristotle, posits that by cultivating specific virtues, individuals can achieve a balanced and ethical life. In this chapter, we will explore how the virtues of patience and humility can be cultivated to help manage anger effectively.

Understanding Virtue Ethics

Virtue ethics is a branch of moral philosophy that emphasizes the development of good character traits, or virtues, as the foundation for ethical behavior. Unlike other ethical theories that focus on rules or consequences, virtue ethics asks, "What kind of person should I be?" rather than "What should I do?"

Aristotle, one of the most influential proponents of virtue ethics, argued that living a virtuous life leads to eudaimonia, often translated as "flourishing" or "the good life." According to Aristotle, virtues are habits or dispositions that enable individuals to act in accordance with reason and achieve moral excellence.

In the context of anger management, virtue ethics suggests that by cultivating virtues such as patience and humility, individuals can regulate their emotional responses, including anger, in a way that promotes harmony and well-being.

The Virtue of Patience

Patience is often described as the ability to endure difficult situations, delays, or challenges without becoming agitated or upset. In virtue ethics, patience is considered a moral virtue that enables individuals to maintain composure and exercise self-control in the face of adversity.

1. Patience as a Moderating Force

Patience acts as a moderating force that helps individuals resist the impulse to react impulsively to provocations. When confronted with a situation that triggers anger, a patient person can pause, reflect, and respond in a measured way rather than reacting with immediate hostility.

- Example: Imagine a parent who is frustrated by their child's constant interruptions while they are trying to work. A patient parent might take a deep breath, acknowledge their child's need for attention, and calmly explain that they will be available shortly, rather than snapping in anger.

Patience allows for a moment of reflection, giving the individual time to assess the situation and choose a response that aligns with their values and goals. By exercising patience, parents can prevent anger from escalating and maintain a positive and supportive relationship with their children.

2. The Role of Patience in Emotional Regulation

Patience is closely linked to emotional regulation, the ability to manage and respond to emotional experiences in a healthy and adaptive way. Cultivating patience involves developing the capacity to tolerate discomfort, delay gratification, and maintain emotional equilibrium.

- Practice: One way to cultivate patience is through mindfulness practices, which encourage individuals to observe their thoughts and emotions without immediate judgment or reaction. By becoming more aware of their emotional states, individuals can develop greater control over their responses to anger triggers.

- Application in Parenting: When dealing with challenging behaviors from children, parents can practice patience by reminding themselves that children are still learning and developing. By approaching situations with patience, parents can model emotional regulation for their children and create an environment of understanding and support.

3. Patience as a Path to Compassion

Patience is also a pathway to compassion, as it allows individuals to put themselves in others' shoes and consider their perspectives. By being patient, one can better understand the motivations and struggles of others, leading to a more empathetic and compassionate response.

- Example: A parent who practices patience might recognize that their child's tantrum is not a deliberate attempt to cause trouble, but rather a result of the child's inability to express their emotions. This understanding can lead to a more compassionate and constructive response, rather than an angry one.

Cultivating patience not only helps in managing anger but also fosters a deeper connection with others, particularly within the family. By approaching situations with patience and compassion, parents can create a more nurturing and supportive environment for their children.

The Virtue of Humility

Humility, another key virtue in virtue ethics, involves recognizing one's limitations, being open to learning, and maintaining a sense of modesty about one's abilities and achievements. In the context of anger management, humility plays a crucial role in mitigating the pride and ego that often fuel anger.

1. Humility as an Antidote to Pride and Ego

Pride and ego are significant contributors to anger. When individuals feel that their pride has been wounded or that they have been disrespected, they may react with anger to defend their sense of self-worth. Humility, by contrast, involves letting go of the need to assert dominance or superiority over others.

- Example: A parent might feel angered when their authority is challenged by a teenager. A humble approach would involve recognizing that the teenager is asserting their growing independence and that this is a natural part of development, rather than taking it as a personal affront.

By cultivating humility, parents can reduce the intensity of their emotional reactions and approach conflicts with a more open and understanding mindset. This allows for more constructive dialogue and problem-solving, rather than escalating anger.

2. Humility and the Willingness to Learn

Humility also involves a willingness to learn from mistakes and accept feedback. In parenting, this means recognizing that no one is perfect and that mistakes are opportunities for growth, rather than occasions for self-criticism or defensiveness.

- Practice: Cultivating humility can involve regularly reflecting on one's actions and being open to feedback from others, including one's children. This might involve asking questions like, "How could I have handled that situation better?" or "What can I learn from this experience?"

- Application in Parenting: When a parent reacts with anger, humility can help them acknowledge their mistake and apologize if necessary. This not only models accountability for children but also fosters a more respectful and trusting relationship.

3. Humility and Forgiveness

Humility is closely related to the ability to forgive, both oneself and others. By letting go of pride and embracing humility, individuals can more easily forgive those who have wronged them, reducing the anger that often accompanies perceived slights or injustices.

- Example: A parent who feels angered by a child's disrespectful behavior can use humility to recognize that the child is still learning and may not fully understand the impact of their actions. This understanding can lead to forgiveness and a focus on teaching, rather than reacting with anger.

Forgiveness, when rooted in humility, helps to dissolve anger and replace it with a sense of peace and acceptance. This creates a more positive and harmonious environment within the family.

The Intersection of Patience and Humility

Patience and humility are interconnected virtues that together create a powerful framework for managing anger. Patience allows individuals to tolerate discomfort and delay reactions, while humility encourages them to let go of pride and embrace a more compassionate and forgiving perspective.

1. The Synergy of Patience and Humility

When practiced together, patience and humility reinforce each other, making it easier to manage anger in a balanced and thoughtful way. Patience provides the space for reflection and understanding, while humility guides the individual toward a response that is grounded in empathy and respect.

- Example: A parent who is patient in the face of a child's misbehavior and humble enough to admit their own shortcomings can approach the situation with a calm and open mind. This leads to a more constructive resolution, rather than an angry confrontation.

2. Cultivating These Virtues Through Practice

Virtue ethics emphasizes that virtues are developed through practice and habituation. This means that cultivating patience and humility requires regular, intentional effort. Over time, these virtues become ingrained in one's character, making it easier to manage anger and respond to challenges with grace and composure.

- Practice: Regularly set aside time for self-reflection, mindfulness, and learning. Engage in activities that challenge your patience and humility, such as dealing with difficult situations or seeking feedback from others.

- Application in Parenting: Encourage your children to develop these virtues as well. Teach them the value of patience by modeling calm responses and the importance of humility by acknowledging your own mistakes and learning from them.

Virtue ethics provides a powerful framework for managing anger through the cultivation of patience and humility. By developing these virtues, individuals can approach challenges with a calm, reflective, and compassionate mindset, reducing the likelihood of anger and promoting healthier relationships.

Patience helps to moderate immediate reactions and allows for thoughtful responses, while humility encourages openness, learning, and forgiveness. Together, these virtues create a foundation for emotional resilience and ethical behavior, both of which are essential for effective anger management.

In the following chapters, we will continue to explore how these and other virtues can be integrated into daily life, offering practical tools and insights for managing anger in the context of parenting and beyond. By cultivating patience and humility, parents can not only manage their own anger but also create a more positive and nurturing environment for their children, leading to a more harmonious and fulfilling family life.

Mindfulness and Reflection

Techniques from Philosophical Traditions that Promote Self-Awareness and Control Over Emotional Responses

Mindfulness and reflection are practices that have been emphasized in various philosophical traditions for centuries as essential tools for achieving self-awareness, emotional regulation, and inner peace. These practices encourage individuals to observe their thoughts, emotions, and reactions with a non-judgmental awareness, allowing them to respond to situations thoughtfully rather than react impulsively. In this chapter, we will explore mindfulness and reflection techniques rooted in different philosophical traditions, focusing on how they can help manage anger and cultivate emotional control.

Mindfulness in Eastern Philosophical Traditions

Mindfulness, as it is commonly understood today, is deeply rooted in Eastern philosophical traditions, particularly Buddhism. In these traditions, mindfulness is seen as a way to cultivate awareness of the present moment, leading to greater clarity, understanding, and emotional balance.

1. Buddhist Mindfulness Practices

In Buddhism, mindfulness (known as sati in Pali) is one of the key components of the Noble Eightfold Path, which is the path to enlightenment and the cessation of suffering. Mindfulness involves being fully present and aware of one's thoughts, emotions, sensations, and surroundings, without becoming attached to them.

- Mindful Breathing: One of the most fundamental mindfulness practices is mindful breathing. By focusing on the breath, individuals can anchor themselves in the present moment, helping to calm the mind and reduce the intensity of emotions like anger.

- Practice: Find a quiet place to sit comfortably. Close your eyes and focus your attention on your breath. Notice the sensation of the air entering and leaving your nostrils, the rise and fall of your chest, and the rhythm of your breathing. If your mind wanders, gently bring your focus back to your breath. This practice can be done for a few minutes each day to cultivate a habit of mindfulness.

- Mindful Observation: This practice involves observing your thoughts and emotions as they arise, without trying to change them or react to them. The goal is to develop a detached awareness that allows you to see your emotions clearly without being overwhelmed by them.

- Practice: Throughout the day, take moments to pause and observe your thoughts and emotions. For example, if you feel anger arising, note it silently: "I am feeling anger." Instead of acting on the anger immediately, observe it as if you were watching clouds pass by in the sky. This helps create a space between the emotion and your reaction, allowing for a more measured response.

2. Taoist Mindfulness and the Concept of Wu Wei

Taoism, another Eastern philosophical tradition, also emphasizes mindfulness and the importance of aligning oneself with the natural flow of life. The concept of wu wei (often translated as "non-action" or "effortless action") is central to Taoist thought and relates closely to mindfulness.

- Wu Wei and Mindfulness: Wu wei is not about inaction, but rather about acting in harmony with the natural world and with one's true self, without forcing or striving. In the context of mindfulness, wu wei encourages individuals to approach life with a sense of ease and awareness, allowing events to unfold naturally without becoming overly attached or reactive.

- Practice: To incorporate wu wei into your mindfulness practice, focus on letting go of the need to control every aspect of your life. During moments of anger or frustration, remind yourself to step back and observe the situation without trying to force a particular outcome. This approach can help reduce the intensity of emotional responses and promote a sense of calm and balance.

Reflection in Western Philosophical Traditions

While mindfulness is often associated with Eastern traditions, reflection is a practice that has been emphasized in Western philosophy, particularly within the Stoic and existentialist traditions. Reflection involves deliberate contemplation of one's thoughts, actions, and emotions, leading to greater self-awareness and intentional living.

1. Stoic Reflection Practices

The Stoic philosophers of ancient Greece and Rome, such as Seneca, Epictetus, and Marcus Aurelius, emphasized the importance of reflection as a means of achieving self-mastery and emotional control. Stoicism teaches that by reflecting on our thoughts and actions, we can align them with reason and virtue, thereby reducing the impact of negative emotions like anger.

- Evening Reflection (Seneca's Practice): Seneca, one of the most prominent Stoic philosophers, recommended the practice of evening reflection, where one reviews the events of the day and considers how they responded to various situations.

- Practice: Before going to bed, take a few minutes to reflect on your day. Ask yourself questions like, "What did I do well today?" "Where did I fall short?" and "How could I have responded differently in moments of anger or frustration?" This practice helps cultivate self-awareness and encourages continuous improvement in managing emotions.

- Premeditatio Malorum (The Pre-Meditation of Evils): Another Stoic practice involves anticipating potential challenges or negative events and reflecting on how to respond to them with virtue and composure.

- Practice: At the start of each day, take a moment to consider potential challenges you might face, such as situations that could provoke anger. Reflect on how you can approach these situations with patience, humility, and emotional control. By preparing your mind in advance, you are better equipped to handle challenges calmly and thoughtfully.

2. Existential Reflection and the Search for Authenticity

Existentialist philosophers, such as Jean-Paul Sartre and Martin Heidegger, emphasized the importance of self-reflection in the quest for authenticity and meaningful living. Existentialism encourages individuals to confront the realities of their existence, including their emotions, and to take responsibility for their actions.

- Authentic Living through Reflection: Existential reflection involves examining one's life, choices, and emotions in the context of one's values and beliefs. By reflecting on the sources of anger and other emotions, individuals can better understand themselves and make choices that align with their true selves.

- Practice: Regularly set aside time to reflect on your emotions, particularly moments of anger. Ask yourself, "What does this anger say about my values or unmet needs?" "Am I living in a way that aligns with my beliefs and goals?" and "How can I address the root causes of my anger to live more authentically?" This type of reflection fosters self-awareness and helps reduce reactive, inauthentic behavior.

Integrating Mindfulness and Reflection into Daily Life

Mindfulness and reflection are complementary practices that, when integrated into daily life, can significantly enhance emotional regulation and self-awareness. Here are some practical strategies for incorporating these practices into your routine:

1. Morning Mindfulness and Reflection Routine

Starting the day with mindfulness and reflection sets a positive tone for the rest of the day. By taking a few minutes each morning to center yourself and reflect on your intentions, you can approach the day with greater clarity and emotional balance.

- Practice: Begin your day with a short mindfulness session, focusing on your breath or simply sitting in silence. Follow this with a brief reflection on what you hope to achieve during the day, how you want to handle potential challenges, and what virtues you want to cultivate. This practice helps you start the day with intention and awareness.

2. Mindful Pauses Throughout the Day

Incorporating mindful pauses into your day helps you stay grounded and aware of your emotional state. These pauses are particularly useful in moments of stress or anger, as they give you the opportunity to reset and respond rather than react.

- Practice: Set an intention to take mindful pauses throughout the day, especially when you notice your emotions becoming intense. During these pauses, take a few deep breaths, observe your thoughts and feelings, and reflect on how you want to proceed. This simple practice can prevent emotional outbursts and promote calm decision-making.

3. Evening Reflection and Journaling

Ending the day with reflection and journaling allows you to process your experiences, learn from them, and prepare for the future. This practice not only helps you understand your emotional responses but also fosters personal growth and emotional resilience.

- Practice: Each evening, spend a few minutes reflecting on the day's events and how you responded to them. Write about moments when you felt anger or other strong emotions, and explore what triggered these feelings, how you managed them, and what you can do differently next time. This practice helps consolidate your learning and reinforces the development of emotional control.

4. Applying Mindfulness and Reflection in Parenting

Mindfulness and reflection are particularly valuable in the context of parenting, where emotions can run high and challenges are frequent. By incorporating these practices into your parenting approach, you can model emotional regulation for your children and create a more peaceful and supportive home environment.

- Practice: When interacting with your children, practice mindful listening—give them your full attention without judgment or distraction. Reflect on your responses to their behavior, and consider whether your reactions align with your values and the example you want to set. Use mindful pauses to collect yourself before addressing challenging behaviors, and reflect on how to approach these situations with patience and understanding.

Mindfulness and reflection, as taught in various philosophical traditions, offer powerful techniques for cultivating self-awareness and emotional control. By integrating these practices into daily life, individuals can manage anger more effectively, respond to challenges with greater composure, and live in alignment with their values.

Mindfulness encourages present-moment awareness and non-judgmental observation of thoughts and emotions, while reflection fosters deep self-examination and intentional living. Together, these practices provide a strong foundation for emotional regulation and personal growth.

As we continue to explore anger management strategies, the insights gained from mindfulness and reflection will serve as essential tools in cultivating a more balanced and fulfilling life. By practicing these techniques regularly, you can develop greater self-awareness, reduce the impact of negative emotions, and create a more harmonious and authentic existence.

Practical Application

Implementing Philosophical Insights into Daily Parenting Practices

Philosophy offers a wealth of insights that can be directly applied to the challenges of parenting. By integrating philosophical principles such as virtue ethics, mindfulness, and reflection into daily parenting practices, parents can cultivate a more thoughtful, balanced, and effective approach to raising their children. This chapter will explore how to practically apply these philosophical insights in everyday parenting situations, helping you to manage your emotions, strengthen your relationships with your children, and create a more harmonious home environment.

1. Cultivating Patience in Daily Interactions

Patience, as discussed in the context of virtue ethics, is a cornerstone of effective parenting. It allows parents to respond to challenges with calmness and understanding rather than anger or frustration. Cultivating patience requires intentional practice and can be integrated into various aspects of daily life.

Strategies for Practicing Patience:

Pause Before Reacting: When your child tests your patience, whether by refusing to follow instructions, throwing a tantrum, or engaging in sibling rivalry, take a moment to pause before reacting. This pause allows you to collect your thoughts, assess the situation calmly, and choose a response that aligns with your values.

- Example: If your child refuses to go to bed, instead of immediately raising your voice, pause and take a deep breath. Reflect on why they might be resisting—are they anxious, overtired, or simply seeking attention? This understanding can help you respond with patience and empathy.

- Mindful Breathing: Incorporate mindful breathing into your daily routine, especially during stressful moments. This simple practice can help you maintain patience by grounding you in the present moment and reducing the physiological responses associated with anger.

- Example: When you feel your patience wearing thin, focus on your breath for a few seconds. Inhale deeply and exhale slowly, allowing the tension to dissipate before you engage with your child.

- Set Realistic Expectations: Recognize that children are still learning and developing, and that mistakes and misbehavior are a normal part of their growth. By setting realistic expectations, you can reduce the frustration that often leads to impatience.

- Example: Instead of expecting your toddler to sit still for an extended period, acknowledge their need for movement and plan activities that accommodate their energy levels. This proactive approach helps prevent situations that could trigger impatience.

2. Practicing Humility in Parenting

Humility, another key virtue, involves recognizing your limitations, being open to learning, and maintaining a sense of modesty about your role as a parent. Humility fosters a nurturing environment where both parents and children can grow together.

Strategies for Practicing Humility:

- Acknowledge Mistakes: Humility involves admitting when you've made a mistake and taking responsibility for it. This not only models accountability for your children but also strengthens your relationship by showing that you are human and willing to learn.

- Example: If you lose your temper and yell at your child, acknowledge the mistake and apologize. Explain that everyone makes mistakes, and use the moment to discuss how you can both handle similar situations better in the future.

- Be Open to Feedback: Children often have valuable perspectives that can teach parents about their needs and preferences. By being open to feedback from your children, you demonstrate humility and a willingness to adapt your parenting style.

- Example: If your child expresses that they feel overwhelmed by too many extracurricular activities, listen to their concerns and consider adjusting their schedule. This openness shows that you value their input and are willing to make changes for their well-being.

- Learn Together: Embrace the idea that parenting is a continuous learning process. Engage in activities that allow you to learn alongside your children, whether it's exploring new hobbies, reading together, or tackling challenges as a team.

- Example: If your child struggles with a particular subject in school, take the opportunity to learn with them.

Work through problems together, showing that it's okay not to have all the answers and that learning is a lifelong journey.

3. Integrating Mindfulness into Parenting

Mindfulness, rooted in Eastern philosophical traditions, emphasizes being fully present and aware in each moment. Integrating mindfulness into your parenting practices can help you manage stress, respond to your children with greater empathy, and create a more peaceful home environment.

Strategies for Practicing Mindfulness:

- Mindful Listening: Practice mindful listening when interacting with your children. Give them your full attention, listen without interrupting, and try to understand their perspective without immediately offering solutions or judgments.

- Example: When your child comes to you with a problem, resist the urge to jump in with advice. Instead, listen attentively, ask open-ended questions, and allow them to express their thoughts fully. This approach fosters better communication and helps your child feel heard and valued.

- Mindful Play: Engage in playtime with your children in a mindful way, focusing entirely on the activity and your connection with them. This not only strengthens your bond but also allows you to experience joy and relaxation together.

- Example: During playtime, set aside distractions like phones or other tasks. Immerse yourself in the activity, whether it's building with blocks, drawing, or playing a game. By being fully present, you enhance the quality of your interactions and create lasting positive memories.

- Modeling Mindfulness: Demonstrate mindfulness in your daily life by showing your children how to approach tasks with focus and calmness. Whether it's preparing meals, doing chores, or handling stress, let your children see how you manage your emotions and stay present.

- Example: If you're feeling stressed while cooking dinner, explain to your child how you're taking deep breaths to stay calm and focused. This modeling teaches them that mindfulness is a practical tool they can use in their own lives.

4. Reflective Parenting Practices

Reflection, emphasized in Stoic and existentialist philosophies, involves taking time to contemplate your actions, thoughts, and emotions. Reflective parenting allows you to learn from your experiences, make intentional changes, and approach challenges with greater wisdom.

Strategies for Reflective Parenting:

- Daily Reflection Time: Set aside time each day to reflect on your parenting experiences. Consider what went well, where you struggled, and how you can improve. This practice helps you stay mindful of your growth as a parent and encourages continuous learning.

- Example: Before bed, spend a few minutes reflecting on the day. Ask yourself, "How did I handle moments of anger or frustration?" "What did I learn about my child today?" and "What can I do differently tomorrow?" This reflection helps you become more intentional in your parenting.

- Journaling: Keep a parenting journal where you document your thoughts, emotions, and experiences. Writing about your reflections can provide clarity, help you track patterns, and serve as a tool for personal growth.

- Example: After a particularly challenging day, write about the events that triggered your anger, how you responded, and what you can learn from the experience. Over time, this journal will become a valuable resource for understanding your emotional responses and improving your parenting strategies.

- Reflecting with Your Child: Engage your child in reflective conversations about their day, emotions, and experiences. This practice not only strengthens your relationship but also teaches your child the value of self-reflection and emotional awareness.

- Example: During dinner or before bed, ask your child reflective questions like, "What was the best part of your day?" "How did you feel when…?" and "What would you do differently next time?" These conversations help your child develop self-awareness and encourage open communication.

5. Applying Philosophical Insights in Conflict Resolution

Conflicts are inevitable in any family, but how they are handled can either escalate tension or foster understanding. By applying philosophical insights such as patience, humility, mindfulness, and reflection, parents can approach conflicts with greater wisdom and effectiveness.

Strategies for Conflict Resolution:

- Approach with Patience: When conflicts arise, approach them with patience, giving yourself and your child time to cool down before addressing the issue. This patience prevents impulsive reactions and allows for a more thoughtful resolution.

- Example: If your child speaks to you disrespectfully, instead of responding immediately, take a moment to breathe and reflect. When you're both calmer, discuss the situation with patience, focusing on understanding the underlying emotions rather than reacting to the words.

- Use Humility to Facilitate Dialogue: Humility in conflict resolution involves recognizing that you may not have all the answers and being open to your child's perspective.

This openness can lead to more collaborative and effective problem-solving.

- Example: During a disagreement about household rules, invite your child to share their thoughts and feelings. Listen with an open mind and be willing to adjust your approach if necessary. This collaborative attitude helps build mutual respect and cooperation.

- Mindful Communication: Practice mindful communication during conflicts by staying present, listening carefully, and avoiding assumptions. This mindful approach reduces misunderstandings and promotes clearer, more effective dialogue.

- Example: If a conflict arises over screen time, engage in a mindful conversation where you listen to your child's viewpoint without interrupting. Respond thoughtfully, expressing your concerns while acknowledging their feelings. This mindful approach helps find a balanced solution that respects both perspectives.

- Reflect and Learn from Conflicts: After a conflict is resolved, take time to reflect on what happened, what you learned, and how you can improve in the future. This reflection helps turn conflicts into opportunities for growth and strengthens your ability to handle future challenges.

- Example: After resolving a conflict, reflect on questions like, "What worked well in our discussion?" "What could I have done differently?" and "How can I apply this experience to future conflicts?" This reflective practice helps you continuously refine your conflict resolution skills.

Philosophical insights, when applied to daily parenting practices, provide a powerful framework for managing emotions, resolving conflicts, and fostering a positive and nurturing family environment. By cultivating virtues such as patience and humility, practicing mindfulness, engaging in reflective parenting, and approaching conflicts with philosophical wisdom, parents can enhance their relationships with their children and create a more harmonious home life.

These practices are not about achieving perfection but about embracing growth, learning, and intentionality in your parenting journey. By integrating these philosophical principles into your daily life, you can navigate the challenges of parenting with greater ease, wisdom, and compassion, ultimately leading to a more fulfilling and joyful experience for both you and your children.

As you continue to explore and apply these insights, remember that philosophy offers a lifelong path to growth and understanding. The more you practice these principles, the more naturally they will become part of your parenting approach, helping you to raise children who are not only well-behaved but also emotionally resilient, thoughtful, and compassionate.

CHAPTER 04

THEOLOGICAL APPROACHES TO ANGER

Biblical Teachings: In-Depth Analysis of Biblical Guidance on Anger

The Bible offers profound insights into human emotions, including anger, providing guidance on how believers can manage and channel this powerful emotion in ways that align with God's will. Biblical teachings emphasize the importance of self-control, the dangers of unchecked anger, and the spiritual significance of patience and forgiveness. In this chapter, we will explore key Biblical passages from the books of Proverbs, Ephesians, and James, analyzing their teachings on anger and how they can be applied in daily life, particularly in the context of parenting.

1. The Wisdom of Proverbs on Anger

The Book of Proverbs, part of the wisdom literature in the Old Testament, offers practical advice on living a righteous and prudent life. Proverbs is filled with teachings on the nature of anger, the consequences of giving in to it, and the virtues that help manage it effectively.

A. The Dangers of Quick Temper and Hasty Words

One of the recurring themes in Proverbs is the warning against being quick-tempered and speaking impulsively out of anger. The wisdom of Proverbs teaches that rashness in anger leads to folly and discord, while restraint and calmness are marks of wisdom.

- Proverbs 14:17: "A quick-tempered person does foolish things, and the one who devises evil schemes is hated."

This verse highlights the folly that often accompanies quick-tempered reactions. Acting out of anger, without taking the time to consider the consequences, often leads to regrettable actions and strained relationships. The "foolish things" mentioned here can range from hasty words to destructive behaviors, all of which can have lasting negative impacts on one's relationships and spiritual well-being.

- Proverbs 15:1: "A gentle answer turns away wrath, but a harsh word stirs up anger."

This verse underscores the power of words in either diffusing or escalating anger. A gentle, calm response can de-escalate a tense situation, while harsh words spoken in anger can inflame tempers further. For parents, this teaching is particularly relevant; responding to a child's disobedience or disrespect with gentle firmness rather than harshness can prevent anger from spiraling out of control.

B. The Value of Patience and Understanding

Proverbs also emphasizes the virtues of patience and understanding in managing anger. These qualities are portrayed as marks of wisdom and strength, enabling individuals to rise above provocation and maintain harmony.

- Proverbs 14:29: "Whoever is patient has great understanding, but one who is quick-tempered displays folly."

Patience is linked with understanding, suggesting that those who take the time to listen, reflect, and consider situations carefully are better equipped to handle anger constructively. In contrast, a quick-tempered person acts without understanding, leading to foolish and often harmful outcomes. For parents, cultivating patience can help them better understand their children's needs and motivations, leading to more effective and compassionate responses.

- Proverbs 16:32: "Better a patient person than a warrior, one with self-control than one who takes a city."

This verse extols the virtue of self-control, comparing it favorably to physical strength or martial prowess. In the biblical worldview, true strength is not about dominating others but about mastering one's own emotions, particularly anger. For parents, this means that exercising self-control, even in the face of provocation, is a sign of true strength and wisdom.

2. Paul's Teachings on Anger in Ephesians

The Apostle Paul's epistle to the Ephesians provides further guidance on how Christians should approach anger, emphasizing the need for self-control, forgiveness, and the avoidance of sin. Paul's teachings offer a blueprint for managing anger in a way that aligns with Christian values and promotes spiritual growth.

A. The Call to Righteous Anger Without Sin

Paul acknowledges that anger is a natural human emotion but warns against allowing it to lead to sin. He emphasizes the importance of dealing with anger promptly and not letting it fester, which can give the devil a foothold in one's life.

- Ephesians 4:26-27: "In your anger do not sin: Do not let the sun go down while you are still angry, and do not give the devil a foothold."

This passage highlights the distinction between righteous anger and sinful anger. While feeling anger is not inherently wrong, it becomes sinful when it leads to actions or thoughts that are contrary to God's will, such as holding grudges, seeking revenge, or speaking hurtful words. Paul's admonition to "not let the sun go down" on anger encourages believers to resolve conflicts quickly, preventing anger from hardening into resentment or bitterness.

For parents, this teaching is especially important in the context of family life. Addressing conflicts and resolving anger before it has time to take root helps maintain peace and unity within the home. It also models for children the importance of reconciliation and forgiveness.

B. The Call to Imitate God's Forgiveness

Paul goes on to exhort believers to be kind and compassionate to one another, forgiving each other just as God forgave them in Christ. This call to forgiveness is central to Christian teaching and is directly connected to how believers should handle anger.

- Ephesians 4:31-32: "Get rid of all bitterness, rage and anger, brawling and slander, along with every form of malice. Be kind and compassionate to one another, forgiving each other, just as in Christ God forgave you."

Here, Paul urges believers to actively rid themselves of negative emotions and behaviors that stem from anger, such as bitterness, rage, and slander. Instead, they are called to embrace kindness, compassion, and forgiveness. This teaching aligns with the Christian understanding of forgiveness as a reflection of God's grace; just as believers have been forgiven, they are called to forgive others.

In parenting, this means that parents should strive to forgive their children's mistakes and misbehaviors, rather than holding onto anger or resentment. By modeling forgiveness, parents can teach their children the value of grace and the importance of letting go of anger.

3. James' Wisdom on Anger and Righteousness

The Epistle of James offers additional insights into the relationship between anger and righteousness, emphasizing the importance of listening, controlling one's tongue, and seeking God's righteousness rather than acting on human anger.

A. The Call to Be Quick to Listen, Slow to Speak, and Slow to Anger

James provides practical advice on how to manage anger by encouraging believers to prioritize listening and thoughtful response over impulsive speech and action.

- James 1:19-20: "My dear brothers and sisters, take note of this: Everyone should be quick to listen, slow to speak and slow to become angry, because human anger does not produce the righteousness that God desires."

This passage highlights the importance of self-restraint in communication. Being "quick to listen" and "slow to speak" helps prevent misunderstandings and allows for more thoughtful and measured responses. By being "slow to anger," believers can avoid the pitfalls of human anger, which, as James notes, does not lead to the righteousness that God desires.

For parents, this teaching is particularly relevant when dealing with conflicts or disciplining their children. Taking the time to listen to their child's perspective before responding can help de-escalate situations and lead to more constructive outcomes. Moreover, controlling anger and responding with calmness and wisdom sets a positive example for children to follow.

B. The Role of Humility in Managing Anger

James also touches on the importance of humility in managing anger, emphasizing that submission to God's will is key to overcoming negative emotions and resisting the devil's temptations.

- James 4:6-7: "But he gives us more grace. That is why Scripture says: 'God opposes the proud but shows favor to the humble.' Submit yourselves, then, to God. Resist the devil, and he will flee from you."

Humility involves recognizing one's limitations and submitting to God's authority. In the context of anger management, humility allows individuals to acknowledge their need for God's grace and guidance in controlling their emotions. By resisting pride and the temptation to act out of anger, believers can align themselves more closely with God's will.

For parents, cultivating humility means acknowledging that they do not have all the answers and that they need God's help in managing their emotions and guiding their children. This humble attitude fosters a spirit of dependence on God and openness to His wisdom, leading to more peaceful and righteous parenting.

The Bible provides a wealth of guidance on how to manage anger in a way that aligns with God's will and promotes spiritual growth. The teachings from Proverbs, Ephesians, and James emphasize the importance of self-control, patience, forgiveness, and humility in dealing with anger. These virtues not only help individuals avoid the pitfalls of sinful anger but also contribute to healthier relationships and a more harmonious life.

For parents, these Biblical teachings offer valuable insights into how to approach the challenges of parenting with wisdom and grace. By applying these principles in daily life, parents can model Christ-like behavior for their children, foster a loving and supportive home environment, and navigate the complexities of family life with greater peace and righteousness.

As you continue to reflect on these teachings, consider how you can integrate them into your own parenting practices. By doing so, you will not only manage your own anger more effectively but also create a legacy of faith, love, and grace that will impact your children for generations to come.

Spiritual Practices

How Prayer, Meditation, and Other Spiritual Practices Can Help Manage Anger

Anger is a powerful emotion that can be difficult to manage, but many spiritual traditions offer practices that can help individuals channel their anger in healthy and constructive ways. Prayer, meditation, and other spiritual practices provide avenues for reflection, self-control, and inner peace, helping to transform anger from a destructive force into an opportunity for personal and spiritual growth. This chapter will explore how these spiritual practices can be used to manage anger, offering practical guidance on incorporating them into daily life.

1. The Power of Prayer in Managing Anger

Prayer is one of the most fundamental spiritual practices across many faith traditions. It serves as a direct line of communication with the divine, offering believers a way to express their emotions, seek guidance, and find solace. When it comes to managing anger, prayer can be a powerful tool for finding calm, gaining perspective, and aligning one's emotions with spiritual values.

A. Types of Prayer for Anger Management

- Petitionary Prayer: This form of prayer involves asking God for help in managing specific emotions, including anger. When feeling overwhelmed by anger, a person might pray for patience, wisdom, and self-control.

- Example: "Lord, please grant me the patience to understand, the wisdom to respond calmly, and the strength to control my anger. Help me to see this situation through Your eyes and to act in a way that honors You."

- Intercessory Prayer: In situations where anger is directed toward another person, intercessory prayer—praying for that individual—can help soften one's heart and foster forgiveness.

- Example: "Lord, I lift up [person's name] to You. Help me to forgive them and to release any anger or resentment I feel. May Your peace fill my heart, and may our relationship be restored."

- Contemplative Prayer: This practice involves quietly sitting in God's presence, allowing oneself to be open to divine guidance and inner peace. Contemplative prayer helps calm the mind and heart, making it easier to let go of anger.

- Example: Find a quiet space, close your eyes, and focus on a simple prayer or word, such as "peace" or "love." Allow yourself to rest in God's presence, letting go of anger and anxiety.

B. The Benefits of Prayer in Managing Anger

- Connection with the Divine: Prayer helps individuals feel connected to a higher power, providing comfort and reassurance during times of emotional turmoil. This connection can bring a sense of calm and perspective, making it easier to manage anger.

- Reflection and Perspective: Prayer offers a moment of pause, allowing individuals to reflect on their emotions and consider how they align with their spiritual beliefs. This reflection can help reframe anger, turning it into an opportunity for growth and understanding.

- Release of Burdens: Prayer provides a way to release the emotional burdens associated with anger. By placing anger in God's hands, individuals can experience a sense of relief and freedom from the weight of their emotions.

2. The Role of Meditation in Anger Management

Meditation is a practice that promotes mindfulness, self-awareness, and inner peace. While often associated with Eastern spiritual traditions, meditation is also present in many other religious contexts. By cultivating a calm and focused mind, meditation can help individuals manage anger more effectively.

A. Types of Meditation for Anger Management

- Mindfulness Meditation: This practice involves observing thoughts and emotions without judgment. When anger arises, mindfulness meditation allows individuals to acknowledge the emotion, understand its source, and let it pass without acting on it impulsively.

- Practice: Find a quiet place to sit comfortably. Close your eyes and focus on your breath. As you meditate, observe any thoughts or emotions that arise, including anger. Notice them without judgment and allow them to pass, returning your focus to your breath.

- Loving-Kindness Meditation (Metta): Loving-kindness meditation focuses on cultivating compassion and goodwill toward oneself and others. This practice can be particularly effective in reducing anger and fostering forgiveness.

- Practice: Sit quietly and bring to mind someone with whom you are angry. Silently repeat phrases such as "May you be happy, may you be healthy, may you be free from suffering." By extending compassion toward the person, you can begin to dissolve feelings of anger.

- Guided Visualization: This form of meditation involves visualizing a peaceful scene or a calming light that helps dissipate anger. Guided visualization can help redirect the mind from anger toward peace and tranquility.

- Practice: Close your eyes and imagine a place where you feel completely at peace, such as a beach or a forest. As you visualize this scene, imagine the anger in your body as a dark cloud. Visualize this cloud dissolving as it is absorbed by the peaceful surroundings, leaving you calm and centered.

B. The Benefits of Meditation in Managing Anger

- Emotional Regulation: Meditation enhances self-awareness and emotional regulation, making it easier to recognize and manage anger before it escalates.

- Increased Patience: Regular meditation practice cultivates patience, helping individuals respond to situations with calmness and understanding rather than anger.

- Stress Reduction: Meditation reduces stress, which is often a precursor to anger. By lowering stress levels, individuals are less likely to react with anger in challenging situations.

3. Other Spiritual Practices for Managing Anger

In addition to prayer and meditation, there are several other spiritual practices that can help individuals manage anger. These practices often involve physical movement, ritual, or community engagement, all of which contribute to emotional balance and spiritual well-being.

A. Practicing Gratitude

Gratitude is a powerful antidote to anger. By focusing on the positive aspects of life and recognizing the blessings that one has, individuals can shift their perspective from frustration and resentment to appreciation and contentment.

- Gratitude Journaling: Keep a daily gratitude journal where you write down things you are thankful for. When anger arises, review your journal to remind yourself of the good in your life.

- Practice: Each evening, write down three things you are grateful for. These can be simple things, such as a kind word from a friend or a beautiful sunset. Reflecting on these blessings can help you maintain a positive outlook and reduce the likelihood of anger taking hold.

- Gratitude Rituals: Incorporate gratitude into your daily routine through simple rituals, such as giving thanks before meals or during moments of quiet reflection.

- Practice: Before each meal, take a moment to silently give thanks for the food and for the people who made it possible. This practice fosters a spirit of gratitude that can counteract feelings of anger and frustration.

B. Engaging in Physical Activity as a Spiritual Practice

Physical activity, when approached mindfully, can be a form of spiritual practice that helps release pent-up anger and restore emotional balance. Many spiritual traditions incorporate movement into their rituals, recognizing the connection between body and spirit.

- Yoga: Yoga is a spiritual practice that combines physical postures, breath control, and meditation. It helps release tension in the body and calm the mind, making it an effective practice for managing anger.

- Practice: Incorporate a regular yoga practice into your routine, focusing on poses that promote relaxation and release stress, such as forward bends and twists. Use your breath to guide your movements and let go of any anger or tension in your body.

- Walking Meditation: Walking meditation is a mindful movement practice that involves walking slowly and intentionally while focusing on each step. This practice helps ground the body and mind, reducing anger and promoting inner peace.

- Practice: Find a quiet place to walk, such as a park or garden. Walk slowly, paying attention to the sensation of your feet touching the ground. With each step, silently repeat a calming word or phrase, such as "peace" or "calm." Allow your anger to dissolve with each step.

C. Rituals and Ceremonies

Rituals and ceremonies, whether religious or personal, can provide structure and meaning in times of emotional turmoil. Engaging in rituals that have personal or spiritual significance can help individuals process and release anger in a sacred and intentional way.

- Candle Lighting: Lighting a candle can be a symbolic act of releasing anger and inviting peace. As the candle burns, it represents the transformation of anger into light and warmth.

- Practice: When you feel anger rising, light a candle and take a few moments to sit quietly. As you watch the flame, imagine your anger being transformed into light, filling you with peace and calm.

- Sacred Space: Creating a sacred space in your home where you can retreat for prayer, meditation, or reflection can provide a sanctuary for managing emotions. This space can be as simple as a corner with a comfortable chair, a candle, and a few meaningful objects.

- Practice: Designate a space in your home as your sacred space. Use this space whenever you need to calm down, pray, or meditate. The familiarity and sanctity of the space will help you find peace and manage anger more effectively.

4. Incorporating Spiritual Practices into Daily Life

To effectively manage anger through spiritual practices, it's important to integrate these practices into your daily routine. Consistency is key to experiencing the full benefits of these practices, as they help build emotional resilience and spiritual strength over time.

A. Establishing a Daily Spiritual Routine

- Morning Rituals: Start your day with a spiritual practice, such as prayer, meditation, or reading a sacred text. This sets a positive tone for the day and helps you approach challenges with a calm and centered mindset.

- Example: Begin each morning with a short prayer or meditation, asking for guidance, patience, and strength to handle whatever comes your way. This practice helps ground you in your spiritual values and prepares you to manage anger effectively.

- Evening Reflection: End your day with a spiritual practice that allows you to reflect on your emotions, release any lingering anger, and find peace before sleep.

- Example: Before bed, take a few minutes to pray or meditate, reflecting on your day and any moments of anger or frustration. Ask for forgiveness if needed, and give thanks for the lessons learned. This practice helps you end the day with a clear mind and a peaceful heart.

B. Using Spiritual Practices in the Moment

In addition to a daily routine, it's important to have spiritual practices that you can use in the moment when anger arises. These practices can help you manage your emotions in real-time, preventing anger from escalating.

- Quick Prayer: When you feel anger rising, say a quick prayer asking for calm and guidance. Even a brief moment of connection with the divine can help shift your perspective and bring a sense of peace.

- Example: Silently say, "Lord, help me to remain calm and respond with love," when you're in a situation that triggers anger. This simple prayer can help you refocus and approach the situation with a more balanced mindset.

- Breathing Meditation: Use breathing meditation to quickly calm your mind and body when anger starts to build. Focus on your breath and let the anger pass with each exhale.

- Example: In the heat of the moment, close your eyes for a few seconds and take three deep breaths. With each exhale, imagine the anger leaving your body and being replaced by calm and clarity.

Spiritual practices such as prayer, meditation, gratitude, physical activity, and rituals offer powerful tools for managing anger. These practices help individuals connect with the divine, cultivate inner peace, and transform anger into opportunities for growth and healing.

By incorporating these spiritual practices into your daily life, you can develop greater self-awareness, emotional resilience, and a deeper connection to your spiritual values.

Whether through prayer, meditation, or other sacred practices, these tools provide a pathway to managing anger in a way that aligns with your faith and leads to a more peaceful and fulfilling life.

As you continue your journey in managing anger, remember that spiritual practices are not just techniques but expressions of your relationship with the divine and your commitment to living a life of love, peace, and compassion. Through these practices, you can navigate the challenges of anger with grace and wisdom, creating a more harmonious and spiritually enriched life for yourself and those around you.

Forgiveness and Reconciliation

The Role of Forgiveness in Reducing Anger and Fostering Healthier Relationships

Forgiveness and reconciliation are central themes in many religious and philosophical traditions, recognized as essential for personal healing, the restoration of relationships, and the cultivation of inner peace. When anger takes hold in relationships—whether between parents and children, spouses, friends, or within communities—it can create deep emotional wounds and lasting discord. However, the practice of forgiveness can break this cycle, reducing anger and paving the way for reconciliation and healthier, more harmonious relationships. This chapter will explore the role of forgiveness in managing anger and how it can foster reconciliation, drawing on spiritual teachings and practical strategies.

1. Understanding Forgiveness

Forgiveness is often misunderstood as condoning or excusing the wrongs done by others. However, true forgiveness is much deeper and more transformative. It involves letting go of resentment and the desire for retribution, and instead, choosing to extend grace, even when it is difficult. Forgiveness is a process that frees both the forgiver and the forgiven, leading to emotional healing and the possibility of restored relationships.

A. Forgiveness as a Process

Forgiveness is not a one-time event but a process that involves several stages:

- Acknowledgment: The first step in forgiveness is acknowledging the hurt and anger you feel. This involves recognizing the impact of the wrong done to you, without minimizing or denying your emotions.

  - Example: A parent who feels deeply hurt by their child's disrespect must first acknowledge their pain and anger before they can begin the process of forgiveness.

  - Decision to Forgive: Forgiveness is a conscious choice. It involves deciding to release the anger and resentment you hold against the person who has wronged you, even if you do not feel ready to forgive fully.

- Example: After acknowledging their anger, the parent might decide, "I choose to forgive my child, even though I am still hurt. I will work on letting go of this resentment."

- Healing: This stage involves the emotional work of letting go, which may include prayer, reflection, or talking through the hurt with someone you trust. It is during this stage that you move from the decision to forgive to actually feeling forgiveness.

- Example: The parent might spend time in prayer, asking for the strength to let go of their anger, or they might discuss their feelings with a trusted friend or counselor.

- Reconciliation: Forgiveness does not always lead to reconciliation, but when it does, it involves rebuilding trust and repairing the relationship. Reconciliation requires both parties to engage in honest communication and to work together to heal the relationship.

- Example: The parent and child might have a heartfelt conversation about the incident, where both express their feelings, apologize, and agree on how to move forward with greater respect and understanding.

B. The Spiritual Foundation of Forgiveness

Forgiveness is deeply rooted in spiritual teachings, particularly in Christianity, where it is seen as a reflection of God's grace. The Bible teaches that as we have been forgiven by God, so we should forgive others.

- Matthew 6:14-15: "For if you forgive other people when they sin against you, your heavenly Father will also forgive you. But if you do not forgive others their sins, your Father will not forgive your sins."

This passage emphasizes the importance of forgiveness in the life of a believer, not just as a moral obligation but as a necessary condition for receiving God's forgiveness. In the context of managing anger, this teaching encourages individuals to practice forgiveness as a way to free themselves from the destructive power of anger and to restore harmony in their relationships.

2. The Role of Forgiveness in Reducing Anger

Anger often stems from a sense of being wronged or hurt. When this anger is left unresolved, it can fester and grow, leading to bitterness, resentment, and even hatred. Forgiveness offers a way to break this cycle, allowing individuals to release the hold that anger has on them and to move toward healing and peace.

A. Releasing Resentment

Resentment is a form of anger that lingers over time, often growing more intense as it is fed by repeated thoughts of the wrongs suffered. Forgiveness helps release this resentment by shifting the focus from the harm done to the possibility of healing.

- Example: A parent who continually resents their child for past misbehaviors might find that their anger spills over into other aspects of their relationship, leading to ongoing tension. By choosing to forgive, the parent can begin to release this resentment, reducing the overall level of anger in the relationship.

B. Letting Go of the Desire for Revenge

The desire for revenge is a common response to being wronged, but it is also one of the most destructive. Seeking revenge perpetuates the cycle of anger and often leads to further harm. Forgiveness, on the other hand, involves letting go of this desire and choosing a path of peace.

- Example: If a parent feels betrayed by their child's dishonesty, they might be tempted to "teach them a lesson" by responding harshly or withholding affection. However, this approach only deepens the hurt on both sides. By forgiving their child, the parent can break the cycle of retribution and open the door to healing.

C. Transforming Anger into Compassion

Forgiveness has the power to transform anger into compassion. When you forgive someone, you begin to see them not just as the person who wronged you, but as a human being with their own struggles, weaknesses, and need for grace.

- Example: A parent who forgives their child for a serious misstep, such as lying or breaking a promise, might come to understand that the child was acting out of fear or insecurity. This understanding can lead to compassion, reducing anger and strengthening the parent-child bond.

3. Forgiveness and Reconciliation in Relationships

While forgiveness is primarily about the individual's internal process of letting go, reconciliation involves restoring the relationship between the parties involved. Forgiveness can occur without reconciliation, but true reconciliation requires both forgiveness and a willingness to rebuild trust.

A. The Process of Reconciliation

Reconciliation is a process that involves several key steps, often beginning with forgiveness but extending into actions that rebuild the relationship.

- Communication: Honest and open communication is essential for reconciliation. Both parties must be willing to express their feelings, listen to each other's perspectives, and address the issues that led to the conflict.

- Example: After a conflict, a parent and child might sit down together to discuss what happened, how it made them feel, and what they can do differently in the future. This conversation is a crucial step in rebuilding trust and understanding.

- Apology and Forgiveness: Apologies play a significant role in reconciliation. An apology acknowledges the harm done and expresses a desire to make amends. When combined with forgiveness, it lays the foundation for rebuilding the relationship.

- Example: If a child apologizes for speaking disrespectfully, and the parent forgives them, this exchange can heal the hurt and restore the relationship. The parent's forgiveness also models the importance of grace and humility for the child.

- Restoring Trust: Trust is often damaged in conflicts, and rebuilding it takes time and consistent effort. Both parties must be committed to making positive changes and to demonstrating reliability and integrity.

- Example: If a child has broken trust by lying, the parent might outline specific steps the child can take to rebuild trust, such as being honest, following through on commitments, and communicating openly. As the child meets these expectations, trust is gradually restored.

B. The Challenges of Reconciliation

Reconciliation is not always easy or straightforward. It requires vulnerability, patience, and a willingness to work through difficult emotions. However, the rewards of reconciliation—peace, restored relationships, and emotional healing—are well worth the effort.

- Overcoming Pride: Pride can be a major obstacle to reconciliation, as it may prevent individuals from admitting their mistakes or seeking forgiveness. Overcoming pride involves humility and a genuine desire to repair the relationship.

- Example: A parent might struggle to apologize to their child after reacting harshly in anger, fearing that it will undermine their authority. However, by setting aside pride and apologizing, the parent models humility and strengthens the parent-child bond.

- Dealing with Deep Wounds: Some conflicts involve deep emotional wounds that take time to heal. Reconciliation in these cases requires ongoing commitment and, often, outside support, such as counseling or mediation.

- Example: In cases of long-standing family conflict, such as estrangement or betrayal, reconciliation may require the help of a therapist or mediator who can facilitate honest communication and help both parties navigate the healing process.

C. The Spiritual Significance of Reconciliation

Reconciliation is more than just resolving a conflict; it is a reflection of divine grace and a core aspect of many spiritual traditions. In Christianity, for example, reconciliation mirrors the relationship between humanity and God, where forgiveness and grace lead to the restoration of fellowship.

- 2 Corinthians 5:18-19: "All this is from God, who reconciled us to himself through Christ and gave us the ministry of reconciliation: that God was reconciling the world to himself in Christ, not counting people's sins against them."

This passage highlights the spiritual importance of reconciliation, not just as a human endeavor but as a divine mandate. Just as God has reconciled humanity to Himself through Christ, believers are called to be agents of reconciliation in their relationships.

- Example: A parent who works to reconcile with a child after a significant conflict is participating in this divine ministry, embodying the principles of forgiveness, grace, and love in their family.

4. Practical Steps for Cultivating Forgiveness and Reconciliation

To make forgiveness and reconciliation a part of your daily life, it's important to adopt practices that encourage these virtues and help you navigate conflicts with grace.

A. Daily Reflection and Prayer

Incorporate daily reflection and prayer into your routine, focusing on forgiveness and reconciliation. This practice can help you stay mindful of unresolved anger and prompt you to take steps toward healing.

- Example: Each evening, spend a few minutes reflecting on any conflicts or lingering anger from the day. Pray for the strength to forgive, the wisdom to reconcile, and the grace to move forward with peace.

B. Developing Empathy

Empathy is crucial for forgiveness and reconciliation. By trying to understand the other person's perspective, you can soften your anger and open your heart to forgiveness.

- Practice: When you feel anger toward someone, take a moment to consider what might have motivated their actions. Reflect on any fears, insecurities, or pressures they might be facing. This practice can help you respond with empathy rather than judgment.

C. Seeking and Offering Apologies

Apologies are powerful tools for healing relationships. Whether you are seeking forgiveness or offering it, an apology can pave the way for reconciliation.

- Practice: When you recognize that you have wronged someone, approach them with a sincere apology. Acknowledge the harm you caused, express regret, and ask for their forgiveness. Likewise, be open to accepting apologies from others and extending forgiveness.

D. Cultivating Patience and Humility

Forgiveness and reconciliation often require patience and humility. By cultivating these virtues, you can approach conflicts with a calm and open heart, making it easier to forgive and reconcile.

- Practice: Work on developing patience and humility in your daily interactions. When conflicts arise, take a step back, breathe deeply, and remind yourself of the bigger picture. This perspective can help you respond with grace and understanding.

Forgiveness and reconciliation are powerful tools for reducing anger and fostering healthier, more fulfilling relationships. While the process of forgiveness can be challenging, it is essential for emotional and spiritual healing. By letting go of resentment, releasing the desire for revenge, and extending grace to others, you can transform anger into compassion and restore harmony in your relationships.

Reconciliation, though not always possible, is the ultimate goal of forgiveness. It involves not just letting go of anger but actively working to rebuild trust and repair the relationship. Through open communication, apologies, and a commitment to change, reconciliation can bring about profound healing and a deeper connection between individuals.

As you incorporate the principles of forgiveness and reconciliation into your life, you will find that your relationships become stronger, your emotional burdens lighter, and your capacity for love and compassion greater. These practices are not just about resolving conflicts but about embracing a way of life that reflects the highest spiritual values—grace, peace, and unity.

By choosing forgiveness and seeking reconciliation, you are not only healing your own heart but also contributing to a more loving and peaceful world.

CHAPTER 05

PSYCHOLOGICAL STRATEGIES FOR ANGER MANAGEMENT

Cognitive-Behavioral Techniques: Tools and Exercises to Change Thought Patterns and Behaviors Related to Anger

Anger is a natural human emotion, but when it becomes overwhelming or uncontrollable, it can lead to significant personal and relational challenges. Cognitive-behavioral techniques (CBT) offer effective tools and exercises for managing anger by addressing the underlying thought patterns and behaviors that fuel it. CBT helps individuals recognize and modify distorted thinking, develop healthier responses, and cultivate behaviors that align with their goals and values. This chapter will explore various cognitive-behavioral techniques that can be used to manage anger, offering practical guidance for incorporating these strategies into daily life.

1. Understanding Cognitive-Behavioral Therapy (CBT) and Its Approach to Anger

Cognitive-behavioral therapy is based on the premise that our thoughts, emotions, and behaviors are interconnected. The way we think about a situation influences how we feel about it, which in turn affects how we respond. By identifying and changing distorted or unhelpful thought patterns, CBT aims to alter emotional responses and promote healthier behaviors.

A. The Cognitive Triangle

The cognitive triangle is a key concept in CBT that illustrates the relationship between thoughts, emotions, and behaviors. When dealing with anger, this model can help individuals understand how their thoughts contribute to their emotional state and behavior.

- Thoughts: These are the beliefs, interpretations, and assumptions we hold about a situation. For example, if someone cuts you off in traffic, you might think, "They did that on purpose to annoy me."

- Emotions: These are the feelings that arise in response to our thoughts. In the traffic example, the thought that someone intentionally cut you off might lead to feelings of anger or frustration.

- Behaviors: These are the actions we take in response to our emotions. Anger might lead you to honk your horn, shout, or drive aggressively.

By intervening at the level of thoughts, CBT seeks to prevent negative emotions and behaviors from escalating.

B. The Role of Cognitive Distortions in Anger

Cognitive distortions are irrational or exaggerated thought patterns that contribute to negative emotions like anger. These distortions can lead to misinterpretations of situations and exacerbate feelings of frustration and hostility.

- Common Cognitive Distortions Related to Anger:

- Catastrophizing: Expecting the worst possible outcome or blowing a situation out of proportion. For example, believing that a minor disagreement with your child means they will never respect you.

- Personalization: Taking things personally, assuming that others' actions are directed at you. For instance, interpreting a colleague's curt response as a personal attack rather than considering that they might be having a bad day.

- Overgeneralization: Making broad, sweeping conclusions based on a single event. For example, thinking,

"My child never listens to me" after they ignore a request once.

- Mind Reading: Assuming you know what others are thinking without evidence. For example, assuming your partner is deliberately trying to provoke you by not doing the dishes.

Identifying these cognitive distortions is the first step in challenging and changing them, leading to healthier emotional responses.

2. Cognitive-Behavioral Techniques for Managing Anger

CBT offers a range of techniques designed to help individuals recognize and modify the thought patterns that contribute to anger. These techniques can be practiced regularly to build emotional resilience and improve anger management.

A. Cognitive Restructuring

Cognitive restructuring, also known as cognitive reframing, involves identifying and challenging distorted thoughts and replacing them with more balanced and realistic ones. This technique helps reduce the intensity of anger by altering the thoughts that fuel it.

- Steps for Cognitive Restructuring:

- Identify the Trigger: Start by identifying the situation that triggered your anger. For example, your child refusing to do their homework.

- Recognize the Thought: Next, identify the specific thought that accompanied the anger. For instance, "My child is being disrespectful on purpose."

- Challenge the Thought: Ask yourself if the thought is accurate and if there might be another way to interpret the situation. For example, consider whether your child might be struggling with the homework rather than being intentionally disrespectful.

- Replace the Thought: Replace the distorted thought with a more balanced and realistic one. For example, "My child might be finding the homework difficult, and that's why they're avoiding it."

- Practice: Regularly practice cognitive restructuring by applying it to different situations where you feel anger. Over time, this can help you develop more constructive thought patterns.

B. Thought Stopping

Thought stopping is a technique used to interrupt and prevent negative thought patterns from escalating. This technique is particularly useful for breaking cycles of rumination that can fuel anger.

- Steps for Thought Stopping:

- Recognize the Thought: When you notice yourself engaging in negative or angry thoughts, consciously acknowledge it. For example, "I'm thinking about how my friend let me down again."

- Use a Stop Signal: Interrupt the thought with a mental or physical signal, such as saying "Stop!" out loud or snapping a rubber band on your wrist. This signal helps break the thought pattern.

- Redirect Your Thoughts: Immediately redirect your thoughts to something neutral or positive. For example, focus on your breathing, recall a happy memory, or think about a task that needs your attention.

- Practice: The more you practice thought stopping, the more automatic it will become. Over time, you'll find it easier to interrupt negative thoughts before they lead to anger.

C. Behavioral Activation

Behavioral activation involves engaging in activities that promote positive emotions and reduce anger. This technique is based on the idea that our behaviors can influence our mood, and by choosing activities that align with our values and goals, we can improve our emotional state.

- Steps for Behavioral Activation:

- Identify Positive Activities: Make a list of activities that bring you joy, relaxation, or a sense of accomplishment.

These might include exercise, hobbies, spending time with loved ones, or engaging in creative pursuits.

- Schedule Activities: Incorporate these activities into your daily or weekly routine, especially during times when you're prone to feeling angry or stressed. For example, schedule a walk in nature after a challenging day at work.

- Track Your Mood: Pay attention to how your mood changes after engaging in positive activities. Notice whether your anger decreases and whether you feel more capable of handling stressful situations.

- Practice: Regularly engaging in behavioral activation can help you build a buffer against anger, making it easier to manage your emotions in difficult situations.

D. Relaxation Techniques

Relaxation techniques are effective for managing the physical symptoms of anger, such as increased heart rate, muscle tension, and shallow breathing. By calming the body, you can reduce the intensity of anger and prevent it from escalating.

- Deep Breathing: Deep breathing involves taking slow, deep breaths to calm the nervous system. Focus on inhaling deeply through your nose, holding the breath for a few seconds, and then exhaling slowly through your mouth.

- Practice: When you feel anger rising, pause and take five deep breaths. Focus on the sensation of the breath entering and leaving your body, allowing yourself to relax with each exhale.

- Progressive Muscle Relaxation: This technique involves tensing and then relaxing each muscle group in the body, starting from the toes and working up to the head. It helps release physical tension associated with anger.

- Practice: Find a quiet place to sit or lie down. Starting with your toes, tense each muscle group for a few seconds, then release the tension while focusing on the sensation of relaxation. Continue this process through your entire body.

- Visualization: Visualization involves imagining a peaceful scene or a calming experience to reduce anger. Picture yourself in a place where you feel safe, calm, and happy, and immerse yourself in the details of that scene.

- Practice: Close your eyes and visualize a calming scene, such as sitting by a tranquil lake or walking through a quiet forest. Focus on the sights, sounds, and sensations of the environment, allowing your mind and body to relax.

E. Problem-Solving Skills

Problem-solving is a cognitive-behavioral technique that helps individuals address the underlying issues that contribute to their anger. By developing effective problem-solving skills, you can reduce frustration and find constructive solutions to challenges.

- Steps for Effective Problem-Solving:

- Identify the Problem: Clearly define the issue that is causing your anger. For example, "I'm angry because my workload is overwhelming."

- Brainstorm Solutions: Generate a list of potential solutions to the problem, without judging their feasibility at this stage. For example, "I could delegate tasks, ask for help, or prioritize my workload."

- Evaluate Solutions: Consider the pros and cons of each solution and choose the one that seems most practical and effective. For example, "Asking for help from a colleague might be the most immediate solution."

- Implement the Solution: Put your chosen solution into action. For example, "I'll talk to my colleague tomorrow and ask for their assistance with this project."

- Evaluate the Outcome: After implementing the solution, assess its effectiveness. If the problem persists, consider trying an alternative solution or adjusting your approach.

- Practice: Regularly practicing problem-solving skills can help you feel more empowered and less overwhelmed, reducing the likelihood of anger.

F. Cognitive Rehearsal

Cognitive rehearsal involves mentally practicing how you will handle challenging situations before they occur. This technique helps prepare you to respond calmly and effectively when faced with potential anger triggers.

- Steps for Cognitive Rehearsal:

- Identify Potential Triggers: Think about situations that are likely to trigger your anger

For example, "I often feel angry when my partner criticizes me."

- Visualize the Situation: Close your eyes and imagine yourself in the triggering situation. Picture it in as much detail as possible.

- Rehearse Your Response: Mentally practice how you will respond to the situation in a calm and constructive manner. For example, "If my partner criticizes me, I'll take a deep breath, listen to what they're saying, and respond with, 'I understand your concern, and I'd like to discuss it calmly.'"

- Repeat: Repeat this mental rehearsal several times, reinforcing the desired response in your mind.

- Practice: By regularly engaging in cognitive rehearsal, you can build confidence in your ability to manage anger and respond effectively to difficult situations.

3. Incorporating Cognitive-Behavioral Techniques into Daily Life

To effectively manage anger, it's important to integrate cognitive-behavioral techniques into your daily routine. Consistent practice helps reinforce new thought patterns and behaviors, making them more automatic over time.

A. Developing a Daily CBT Routine

- Morning Reflection: Start your day with a brief reflection on your goals and intentions. Consider any potential challenges and mentally rehearse how you will handle them using CBT techniques.

- Example: "Today, I'll focus on staying calm during stressful meetings. If I feel anger rising, I'll use deep breathing and cognitive restructuring to stay grounded."

- Midday Check-In: Take a few minutes during the day to check in with yourself. Assess your emotional state and practice a CBT technique if needed, such as cognitive restructuring or thought stopping.

- Example: "I'm feeling frustrated after that conversation. I'll take a moment to challenge my thoughts and reframe the situation."

- Evening Review: End your day with a review of how you managed your emotions. Reflect on what worked well and identify areas for improvement.

- Example: "I handled that disagreement calmly, but I could have used deep breathing more effectively. I'll practice that technique more."

B. Using CBT Techniques in the Moment

In addition to a daily routine, it's important to have CBT techniques that you can use in the moment when anger arises. These techniques can help you manage your emotions in real-time and prevent anger from escalating.

- Quick Cognitive Restructuring: When you notice anger starting to build, quickly identify and challenge any distorted thoughts. Replace them with a more balanced perspective.

- Example: "I'm thinking that my colleague is ignoring me, but they might just be busy. I'll give them the benefit of the doubt."

- Immediate Thought Stopping: Use thought stopping as soon as you recognize a negative thought pattern. Redirect your thoughts to something neutral or positive.

- Example: "I'm dwelling on that argument. Stop. I'll focus on my breath instead."

- On-the-Spot Relaxation: Practice deep breathing or progressive muscle relaxation in the moment to calm your body and mind.

- Example: "I'm feeling tense. I'll take five deep breaths to relax."

Cognitive-behavioral techniques offer powerful tools for managing anger by addressing the underlying thought patterns and behaviors that fuel it. By practicing cognitive restructuring, thought stopping, behavioral activation, relaxation techniques, problem-solving skills, and cognitive rehearsal, you can develop healthier emotional responses and reduce the impact of anger on your life.

Incorporating these techniques into your daily routine helps reinforce positive changes and builds emotional resilience. Whether you're dealing with everyday stressors or more significant challenges, CBT provides practical strategies for managing anger and promoting a more peaceful and fulfilling life.

As you continue to practice these techniques, remember that change takes time. Be patient with yourself, and celebrate the progress you make along the way. With consistent effort, you can transform your relationship with anger and create a more balanced and harmonious life.

Stress Management

Techniques to Manage Stress That Often Exacerbates Anger, Such as Relaxation Exercises and Time Management

Stress is a common trigger for anger, often exacerbating emotional responses and making it difficult to maintain control in challenging situations. Managing stress effectively is therefore crucial in reducing the likelihood of anger and improving overall emotional well-being. This chapter will explore various techniques for managing stress, including relaxation exercises, time management strategies, and other practical approaches to creating a more balanced and peaceful life.

1. Understanding the Connection Between Stress and Anger

Stress and anger are closely related emotions. When stress levels rise, the body's fight-or-flight response is activated, which can make a person more prone to anger. Stress can also deplete emotional resources, leaving individuals less capable of coping with frustrations and more likely to react with anger.

A. The Physiological Effects of Stress

Stress triggers a series of physiological responses in the body, including the release of stress hormones like cortisol and adrenaline. These hormones prepare the body to respond to perceived threats by increasing heart rate, blood pressure, and muscle tension. While these responses are useful in emergency situations, they can also lead to heightened emotional reactivity, including anger, when triggered by non-threatening stressors.

B. The Psychological Impact of Stress

Psychologically, stress can lead to feelings of overwhelm, frustration, and irritability. When stress is chronic or unmanaged, it can lower an individual's tolerance for frustration, making them more susceptible to anger. This can create a vicious cycle where stress leads to anger, which in turn creates more stress.

2. Relaxation Exercises to Manage Stress

Relaxation exercises are effective tools for reducing the physiological and psychological effects of stress. By calming the body and mind, these exercises help lower stress levels, making it easier to manage anger and other strong emotions.

A. Deep Breathing

Deep breathing is one of the simplest and most effective relaxation techniques. It involves taking slow, deep breaths to activate the body's relaxation response, counteracting the effects of stress.

- Steps for Deep Breathing:

- Find a Quiet Space: Sit or lie down in a comfortable position in a quiet environment.

- Inhale Deeply: Slowly inhale through your nose, allowing your abdomen to expand as you fill your lungs with air. Count to four as you inhale.

- Hold Your Breath: Hold the breath for a count of four, allowing the oxygen to circulate through your body.

- Exhale Slowly: Exhale slowly through your mouth, counting to four as you release the air. Focus on the sensation of the breath leaving your body and feel the tension dissipate.

- Repeat: Continue this breathing pattern for several minutes, focusing on the rhythm of your breath and the calming effect it has on your body and mind.

B. Progressive Muscle Relaxation (PMR)

Progressive muscle relaxation involves tensing and then slowly relaxing each muscle group in the body. This technique helps release physical tension and promotes a deep state of relaxation.

- Steps for Progressive Muscle Relaxation:

- Get Comfortable: Sit or lie down in a comfortable position in a quiet space.

- Start with Your Feet: Begin by tensing the muscles in your feet. Hold the tension for five to ten seconds, then release it slowly. Focus on the sensation of relaxation as the tension leaves your muscles.

- Move Up the Body: Gradually work your way up the body, tensing and relaxing each muscle group—calves, thighs, abdomen, chest, arms, hands, shoulders, neck, and face.

- Breathe Deeply: As you release each muscle group, take a deep breath and exhale slowly. This will enhance the relaxation response.

- Complete the Process: Once you have relaxed each muscle group, take a few moments to enjoy the sensation of relaxation throughout your body.

C. Guided Imagery

Guided imagery involves visualizing a peaceful and calming scene to help reduce stress and promote relaxation. This technique can be particularly effective in managing stress-related anger by providing a mental escape from stressful situations.

- Steps for Guided Imagery:

- Choose a Peaceful Scene: Think of a place where you feel completely relaxed and safe, such as a beach, forest, or mountain retreat.

- Close Your Eyes: Find a quiet place to sit or lie down, and close your eyes.

- Visualize the Scene: Imagine yourself in the peaceful scene you've chosen. Use all your senses to make the scene as vivid as possible—see the colors, hear the sounds, feel the textures, and even smell the scents.

- Stay in the Scene: Spend several minutes fully immersed in your imagined environment. Allow yourself to feel the calm and relaxation that this scene brings.

- Return Slowly: When you're ready, slowly bring your attention back to the present moment, carrying the sense of peace and relaxation with you.

D. Mindfulness Meditation

Mindfulness meditation involves focusing on the present moment without judgment. This practice helps reduce stress by promoting awareness and acceptance of your thoughts and feelings, rather than reacting to them impulsively.

- Steps for Mindfulness Meditation:

- Find a Quiet Space: Sit comfortably in a quiet space with your eyes closed.

- Focus on Your Breath: Begin by focusing on your breath. Notice the sensation of the air entering and leaving your body.

- Observe Your Thoughts: As you meditate, thoughts and feelings will naturally arise. Rather than getting caught up in them, simply observe them as they come and go, like clouds passing in the sky.

- Return to the Breath: If you find your mind wandering, gently bring your focus back to your breath.

- Practice Regularly: Aim to practice mindfulness meditation for 10 to 20 minutes each day. Over time, this practice can help you develop a greater sense of calm and resilience in the face of stress.

3. Time Management Techniques to Reduce Stress

Effective time management is a critical component of stress management. When time is managed well, it reduces the pressure and overwhelm that can lead to stress and anger. By organizing your tasks and responsibilities more effectively, you can create a more balanced and manageable schedule.

A. Prioritization

Prioritizing tasks helps you focus on what is most important and ensures that your time and energy are spent on activities that align with your goals and values.

- Steps for Prioritization:

- Make a List: Begin by listing all the tasks you need to accomplish. This can include work responsibilities, household chores, personal goals, and social commitments.

- Rank the Tasks: Once you have your list, rank each task based on its importance and urgency. Consider what tasks will have the most significant impact if completed and which ones can be postponed or delegated.

- Focus on High-Priority Tasks: Start your day by tackling the high-priority tasks. This ensures that the most critical activities are completed, reducing stress and preventing last-minute rushes.

B. Time Blocking

Time blocking is a technique that involves scheduling specific blocks of time for different tasks or activities. This method helps create structure in your day and ensures that each task receives the attention it needs.

- Steps for Time Blocking:

- Identify Key Activities: List the main tasks or activities you need to complete each day or week.

- Allocate Time Blocks: Assign specific blocks of time to each task or activity. Be realistic about how much time each task will take and include buffer time for breaks or unexpected interruptions.

- Stick to the Schedule: Once you've created your time blocks, do your best to stick to them. Avoid multitasking and focus on the task at hand during its designated time.

- Review and Adjust: At the end of each day or week, review your schedule to see what worked well and where you might need to make adjustments.

C. The Pomodoro Technique

The Pomodoro Technique is a time management method that involves working in short, focused intervals, followed by short breaks. This technique can help reduce stress by breaking tasks into manageable segments and preventing burnout.

- Steps for the Pomodoro Technique:

- Choose a Task: Select a task that you need to work on.

- Set a Timer: Set a timer for 25 minutes (this is one "Pomodoro").

- Work on the Task: Focus solely on the task for the full 25 minutes, avoiding any distractions.

- Take a Short Break: When the timer goes off, take a 5-minute break. Use this time to relax, stretch, or clear your mind.

- Repeat the Cycle: After four Pomodoros, take a longer break of 15-30 minutes. This cycle helps maintain focus and productivity while allowing regular rest to prevent stress.

D. Delegation and Saying No

Delegating tasks and learning to say no are essential time management skills that help reduce stress. By recognizing your limits and sharing responsibilities, you can prevent overload and maintain a healthier balance.

- Steps for Delegation and Saying No:

- Identify Tasks to Delegate: Review your tasks and identify which ones can be delegated to others. Consider your strengths and the strengths of those around you, and delegate tasks accordingly.

- Communicate Clearly: When delegating, communicate clearly about what needs to be done, the expected outcome, and the deadline. Provide any necessary support or guidance.

- Practice Saying No: Recognize when your schedule is full and practice saying no to additional commitments. It's important to protect your time and energy, especially when taking on more would lead to stress and overwhelm.

- Set Boundaries: Establish clear boundaries around your time, such as limiting the number of projects you take on or setting specific work hours. This helps you stay focused and prevents overcommitment.

4. Lifestyle Changes to Support Stress Management

In addition to specific techniques, certain lifestyle changes can help manage stress more effectively, creating a foundation for emotional well-being and reducing the likelihood of anger.

A. Regular Physical Activity

Exercise is one of the most effective ways to reduce stress and improve mood. Physical activity releases endorphins, the body's natural "feel-good" chemicals, which help counteract the effects of stress.

- Incorporate Exercise into Your Routine: Aim for at least 30 minutes of moderate exercise most days of the week. This could include activities like walking, running, cycling, swimming, or yoga. Regular exercise not only helps reduce stress but also boosts energy levels and enhances overall health.

B. Healthy Eating

Nutrition plays a significant role in managing stress. A balanced diet provides the energy and nutrients your body needs to cope with stress effectively.

- Eat a Balanced Diet: Focus on eating a variety of whole foods, including fruits, vegetables, whole grains, lean proteins, and healthy fats. Avoid excessive caffeine, sugar, and processed foods, which can exacerbate stress and contribute to mood swings.

C. Adequate Sleep

Sleep is crucial for stress management. Lack of sleep can increase stress levels, impair cognitive function, and reduce emotional resilience.

- Prioritize Sleep: Aim for 7-9 hours of quality sleep each night. Establish a regular sleep schedule, create a relaxing bedtime routine, and make your sleep environment conducive to rest (e.g., a cool, dark, and quiet room).

D. Social Support

Maintaining strong social connections is essential for managing stress. Supportive relationships provide emotional comfort, practical help, and a sense of belonging, all of which can buffer against stress.

- Cultivate Relationships: Make time to connect with friends, family, and loved ones regularly. Share your feelings and experiences, and seek support when needed. Building and maintaining a strong support network can help you navigate stressful situations more effectively.

5. Integrating Stress Management Techniques into Daily Life

To effectively manage stress and reduce anger, it's important to integrate these techniques into your daily life. Consistent practice helps build resilience and creates a more balanced and peaceful lifestyle.

A. Create a Daily Routine

Incorporate stress management techniques into your daily routine to ensure that they become a regular part of your life.

- Morning Routine: Start your day with a relaxation exercise, such as deep breathing or mindfulness meditation, to set a calm and focused tone for the day.

- Midday Check-In: Take a few moments during the day to practice a relaxation exercise or review your time management plan. This helps you stay on track and manage any emerging stress.

- Evening Wind-Down: End your day with a relaxing activity, such as guided imagery or progressive muscle relaxation, to release the stress of the day and prepare for restful sleep.

B. Practice Mindfulness Throughout the Day

In addition to formal relaxation exercises, practice mindfulness throughout the day by staying present and fully engaged in each moment.

- Mindful Breathing: When you feel stress rising, pause and take a few deep breaths. Focus on the sensation of the breath entering and leaving your body, and let go of any tension or worry.

- Mindful Eating: Practice mindfulness during meals by paying attention to the flavors, textures, and aromas of your food. This helps you stay grounded and reduces stress-related overeating.

C. Regularly Review and Adjust Your Time Management Plan

Time management is an ongoing process that requires regular review and adjustment. Make it a habit to assess your schedule and make necessary changes to maintain balance and reduce stress.

- Weekly Review: At the end of each week, review your time management plan. Reflect on what worked well, where you encountered stress, and how you can improve for the following week.

Effective stress management is crucial for reducing anger and improving overall emotional well-being. By incorporating relaxation exercises, time management strategies, and other lifestyle changes into your daily routine, you can create a more balanced and peaceful life.

Stress is an inevitable part of life, but with the right tools and techniques, you can manage it effectively and prevent it from leading to anger. By practicing these techniques regularly, you'll build resilience, improve your ability to cope with challenges, and create a foundation for long-term emotional health.

Remember that managing stress is an ongoing process. Be patient with yourself as you develop these skills, and celebrate the progress you make along the way. With consistent effort, you can transform your relationship with stress and create a more harmonious and fulfilling life.

Effective Communication

Strategies for Communicating Effectively with Children and Resolving Conflicts Constructively

Effective communication is the foundation of healthy relationships, particularly between parents and children. It enables parents to convey their expectations, understand their children's needs and feelings, and resolve conflicts in a constructive manner. When communication breaks down, misunderstandings and frustration can escalate, leading to conflicts that may foster resentment and hinder the parent-child relationship. In this chapter, we will explore strategies for communicating effectively with children, with a focus on resolving conflicts in ways that promote understanding, respect, and emotional well-being.

1. The Importance of Effective Communication in Parenting

Effective communication involves more than just exchanging words; it's about connecting with your child on an emotional level, understanding their perspective, and expressing your thoughts and feelings clearly and respectfully. Good communication fosters trust, strengthens bonds, and helps children develop critical social and emotional skills.

A. Building Trust and Understanding

When parents communicate openly and effectively with their children, it creates an environment of trust and mutual respect. Children who feel heard and understood are more likely to be open and honest with their parents, which is crucial for navigating the challenges of childhood and adolescence.

- Consistency and Honesty: Being consistent in your words and actions and being honest with your children helps build trust. Children need to know that they can rely on their parents to be truthful and dependable.

- Empathy: Understanding your child's feelings and perspectives, even when they differ from your own, helps to build a strong emotional connection. Empathy in communication shows that you value and respect your child's experiences.

B. Teaching by Example

Parents are role models for their children, and the way you communicate sets an example for how your children will communicate with others. By practicing effective communication, you teach your children how to express themselves, listen to others, and resolve conflicts respectfully.

- Modeling Good Communication: Use clear, respectful language when speaking with your children and others. Demonstrate active listening, and show how to navigate disagreements with calmness and respect.

- Encouraging Open Dialogue: Create a home environment where open communication is encouraged. Let your children know that they can come to you with any issue, and that their thoughts and feelings will be respected.

2. Strategies for Effective Communication with Children

To communicate effectively with children, parents need to employ strategies that are age-appropriate, empathetic, and clear. The following strategies will help you engage in meaningful conversations with your children and address conflicts constructively.

A. Active Listening

Active listening is a critical component of effective communication. It involves fully focusing on what the other person is saying, without interrupting, judging, or preparing a response while they are speaking. Active listening shows your child that you value their thoughts and feelings.

- Steps for Active Listening:

- Give Full Attention: Make eye contact, put away distractions like phones or the television, and focus entirely on your child.

- Reflect Back What You Hear: After your child speaks, paraphrase what they've said to confirm your understanding. For example, "So, you're upset because your friend didn't invite you to the party?"

- Ask Open-Ended Questions: Encourage your child to share more by asking open-ended questions. For example, "How did that make you feel?" or "What do you think we can do about it?"

- Validate Their Feelings: Acknowledge your child's emotions without dismissing or minimizing them. For example, "I can see why you would feel sad about that. It's okay to feel that way."

B. Clear and Age-Appropriate Language

Using language that is clear, concise, and appropriate for your child's age and developmental stage is crucial in ensuring that they understand what you're saying. Complex words or concepts can confuse younger children, leading to misunderstandings.

- Adjusting Language to Age:

- Young Children: Use simple, concrete language and short sentences. For example, instead of saying, "It's important to be considerate of others' feelings," say, "It's nice to be kind to your friends."

- Older Children and Teens: You can use more complex language, but be clear and direct. For example, "I understand that you want more independence, but let's talk about how we can balance that with your responsibilities."

- Being Specific: Avoid vague language and be specific about what you expect or need. For example, instead of saying, "Behave yourself," say, "Please speak politely when you're upset."

C. Using "I" Statements

"I" statements are a way of expressing your feelings and needs without blaming or criticizing the other person. This approach can help prevent defensiveness and promote more productive communication.

- How to Use "I" Statements:

- State Your Feelings: Begin with "I feel…" to express how you're feeling. For example, "I feel frustrated…"

- Describe the Behavior: Follow with a description of the behavior that's causing the feeling. For example, "…when you don't listen to what I'm saying."

- Explain the Impact: Explain the impact of the behavior on you or the situation. For example, "…because it makes it harder for us to solve the problem together."

- Suggest a Solution: End with a suggestion for how to address the issue. For example, "Let's work together to make sure we both listen to each other."

- Example of an "I" Statement: "I feel upset when you don't do your homework because I worry about your grades. Let's set a time to work on it together."

D. Positive Reinforcement

Positive reinforcement involves acknowledging and rewarding desirable behaviors to encourage them in the future. This approach helps build self-esteem and motivates children to communicate and behave in positive ways.

- Examples of Positive Reinforcement:

- Praise Specific Behaviors: Instead of giving general praise, be specific about what your child did well. For example, "I'm really proud of how you stayed calm and explained your feelings during our talk."

- Use Rewards Sparingly: Occasionally, tangible rewards like a special treat or extra playtime can be used to reinforce positive behavior, but it's important not to rely on rewards too heavily. The goal is to help your child internalize positive behaviors.

- Encourage Effort: Praise your child's effort, not just the outcome. For example, "I can see you worked really hard on that project, and I'm proud of your dedication."

E. Managing Emotions During Communication

Emotions can run high during conflicts, making it difficult to communicate effectively. It's important to manage your emotions and help your child do the same to keep the conversation productive.

- Strategies for Managing Emotions:

- Take a Break: If emotions are escalating, suggest taking a short break to cool down before continuing the conversation. For example, "Let's take a few minutes to calm down and then we'll talk about this."

- Use Calming Techniques: Practice deep breathing or mindfulness exercises together to reduce stress and tension before discussing a difficult topic.

- Stay Calm: Model calm behavior for your child by speaking in a steady tone and avoiding raised voices. This sets the tone for a more respectful and constructive conversation.

- Teaching Emotional Regulation:

- Help Your Child Name Their Emotions: Encourage your child to identify and express their emotions. For example, "It sounds like you're feeling really frustrated right now. Do you want to talk about it?"

- Discuss Healthy Ways to Express Emotions: Teach your child appropriate ways to express their emotions, such as using "I" statements, talking about their feelings, or engaging in calming activities.

F. Setting Clear Expectations and Boundaries

Clear expectations and boundaries help prevent misunderstandings and reduce conflicts. When children know what is expected of them and what the limits are, they are more likely to follow rules and communicate openly.

- How to Set Expectations and Boundaries:

- Be Clear and Specific: Clearly communicate your expectations and the reasons behind them. For example, "You need to finish your homework before playing video games because schoolwork is important for your learning."

- Involve Your Child: Involve your child in setting some of the rules and expectations. This gives them a sense of ownership and responsibility. For example, "Let's agree on a reasonable bedtime that works for both of us."

- Consistent Enforcement: Be consistent in enforcing rules and boundaries. Inconsistency can lead to confusion and increased conflict.

- Example of Setting Boundaries: "It's important that you're home by 9 PM on school nights. If you're late, there will be a consequence, like losing your phone privileges for the next day."

3. Strategies for Resolving Conflicts Constructively

Conflicts are a natural part of any relationship, but how they are handled can make a significant difference in the outcome. Constructive conflict resolution involves addressing the issue at hand while preserving the relationship and maintaining mutual respect.

A. Staying Focused on the Issue

When resolving conflicts, it's important to stay focused on the specific issue rather than bringing up past grievances or generalizing the problem.

- How to Stay Focused:

- Address One Issue at a Time: Focus on the current conflict and avoid bringing up unrelated issues. For example, if the conflict is about screen time, avoid discussing unrelated topics like chores or school performance.

- Avoid Generalizations: Use specific examples rather than making broad statements. For example, instead of saying, "You never listen to me," say, "Yesterday, when I asked you to turn off the TV, you kept watching it."

- Stay in the Present: Focus on resolving the issue at hand rather than rehashing past conflicts. This helps prevent the conversation from becoming overwhelming or unproductive.

B. Finding Common Ground

Finding common ground involves identifying shared goals or values that both you and your child can agree on. This creates a foundation for resolving the conflict collaboratively.

- Steps for Finding Common Ground:

- Identify Shared Goals: Start by discussing what both of you want to achieve. For example, "We both want to make sure you get enough sleep so you're not tired at school."

- Explore Solutions Together: Brainstorm possible solutions that address both your needs and your child's. For example, "What if we agree on a bedtime that gives you enough sleep but also gives you some time to relax before bed?"

- Compromise: Be willing to make compromises that respect both your boundaries and your child's needs. For example, "You can stay up 30 minutes later on weekends, but during the week, we'll stick to the usual bedtime."

C. Using Problem-Solving Techniques

Problem-solving techniques help turn conflicts into opportunities for learning and growth. By approaching conflicts as problems to be solved together, you can model constructive conflict resolution for your child.

- Steps for Problem-Solving:

- Define the Problem: Clearly define the problem and agree on what needs to be resolved. For example, "We need to figure out a way to manage screen time so it doesn't interfere with homework."

- Brainstorm Solutions: Work together to brainstorm possible solutions without judging them at first. Encourage creativity and open-mindedness.

- Evaluate Solutions: Discuss the pros and cons of each solution and choose the one that seems most practical and fair.

- Implement the Solution: Put the chosen solution into action and agree on a plan for how it will be implemented.

- Review the Outcome: After some time, review how the solution is working and make adjustments if needed. For example, "How do you feel about the new screen time rules? Are they helping you focus better on your homework?"

D. Apologizing and Forgiving

Apologies and forgiveness are essential components of resolving conflicts and restoring relationships. They help repair the emotional damage caused by conflicts and allow both parties to move forward.

- Steps for Apologizing:

- Acknowledge the Hurt: Begin by acknowledging the hurt or harm caused by your actions. For example, "I'm sorry that I raised my voice earlier. I know it hurt your feelings."

- Take Responsibility: Accept responsibility for your actions without making excuses. For example, "I shouldn't have yelled, even though I was frustrated."

- Make Amends: Offer to make amends or discuss how to prevent the issue from happening again. For example, "Next time, I'll try to stay calm. Can we agree to talk things through instead of shouting?"

- Encouraging Forgiveness:

- Model Forgiveness: Show your child how to forgive by forgiving them when they make mistakes and asking for their forgiveness when needed.

- Discuss the Importance of Letting Go: Talk about the importance of letting go of anger and resentment for the sake of the relationship. For example, "Holding onto anger only makes us both feel bad. Let's try to move past this together."

- Example of an Apology and Forgiveness: "I'm sorry for getting angry earlier. I know I hurt your feelings, and I didn't mean to. Can you forgive me? Let's work on talking things through calmly next time."

4. Overcoming Communication Barriers

Communication barriers can hinder effective communication and conflict resolution. Identifying and addressing these barriers is crucial for maintaining a healthy parent-child relationship.

A. Addressing Defensive Reactions

Defensiveness can prevent productive communication by causing both parties to shut down or become confrontational. It's important to recognize and address defensive reactions to keep the conversation constructive.

- How to Address Defensiveness:

- Stay Calm: If you notice defensiveness, stay calm and avoid escalating the situation. Use a soft tone and reassuring language.

- Acknowledge Feelings: Acknowledge your child's feelings without judgment. For example, "I can see that you're upset, and that's okay. Let's talk about what's bothering you."

- Refocus the Conversation: Gently steer the conversation back to the issue at hand and emphasize that you're on the same team. For example, "We're both trying to figure this out together, and I'm here to help."

B. Dealing with Avoidance

Some children may avoid communication or conflict altogether, either by shutting down, walking away, or refusing to talk. It's important to address avoidance in a way that encourages open dialogue.

- How to Deal with Avoidance:

- Create a Safe Space: Ensure your child feels safe and comfortable expressing themselves. Let them know that it's okay to talk about difficult topics and that you're there to listen, not to judge or punish.

- Be Patient: If your child avoids a conversation, give them some time and space, but follow up later. For example, "I noticed you didn't want to talk earlier. When you're ready, I'm here to listen."

- Encourage Gradual Communication: Start with small, non-threatening conversations to build your child's comfort level with communication. Gradually work up to more difficult topics.

C. Navigating Cultural and Generational Differences

Cultural and generational differences can sometimes create communication challenges, particularly in families where parents and children have different experiences or perspectives.

- How to Navigate Cultural and Generational Differences:

- Educate Yourself: Learn about the cultural or generational differences that may influence your child's perspective. This knowledge can help you approach conversations with greater understanding and empathy.

- Respect Differences: Acknowledge and respect the differences in perspectives, even if you don't always agree. For example, "I know that your experiences are different from mine, and I want to understand where you're coming from."

- Find Common Ground: Focus on shared values and goals that transcend cultural or generational differences. For example, "We both want what's best for you, so let's work together to find a solution that works for both of us."

5. Encouraging Ongoing Communication and Growth

Effective communication is an ongoing process that requires regular attention and effort. By encouraging continuous communication and personal growth, you can strengthen your relationship with your child and navigate conflicts more effectively.

A. Regular Check-Ins

Regular check-ins provide an opportunity to maintain open communication and address any emerging issues before they escalate into conflicts.

- How to Conduct Regular Check-Ins:

- Schedule Consistent Times: Set aside regular times for check-ins, such as once a week during family dinners or before bedtime.

- Ask Open-Ended Questions: Use open-ended questions to encourage your child to share their thoughts and feelings. For example, "What's been on your mind lately?" or "How are you feeling about school?"

- Listen and Respond: Actively listen to your child's responses and provide support or guidance as needed. Use check-ins as an opportunity to reinforce positive behaviors and address any concerns.

B. Encouraging Personal Growth and Self-Expression

Encouraging your child to grow and express themselves can help them develop the confidence and communication skills needed to navigate conflicts effectively.

- How to Encourage Personal Growth:

- Support Interests and Hobbies: Encourage your child to pursue activities and hobbies that interest them. This helps build their self-esteem and provides opportunities for self-expression.

- Promote Emotional Literacy: Teach your child about different emotions and how to express them in healthy ways. For example, use books, games, or discussions to explore emotions and their impact on behavior.

- Encourage Independence: Allow your child to take on age-appropriate responsibilities and make decisions for themselves. This fosters a sense of autonomy and helps them develop problem-solving skills.

C. Creating a Positive Communication Culture

Creating a positive communication culture in your home involves setting the tone for how communication is handled and ensuring that everyone feels valued and heard.

- How to Create a Positive Communication Culture:

- Set Communication Expectations: Establish family communication rules, such as speaking respectfully, listening to each other, and addressing conflicts calmly.

- Celebrate Successes: Acknowledge and celebrate when effective communication and conflict resolution lead to positive outcomes. For example, "I'm proud of how we worked through that problem together."

- Foster a Safe Environment: Ensure that your home is a safe space where everyone feels comfortable expressing themselves without fear of judgment or retaliation.

Effective communication is the cornerstone of a healthy parent-child relationship and is essential for resolving conflicts constructively. By practicing active listening, using clear and age-appropriate language, and employing problem-solving techniques, you can create an environment where your child feels valued, understood, and respected.

Communication is a skill that requires ongoing attention and practice. As you continue to develop these strategies, you will not only improve your ability to communicate with your child but also strengthen your relationship and build a foundation for navigating future challenges together.

Remember that effective communication is a two-way process. By being open, empathetic, and patient, you can foster a relationship based on trust and mutual respect, where conflicts are seen as opportunities for growth rather than sources of division. With these tools, you can create a more harmonious and fulfilling family life, where both you and your child feel heard, supported, and connected.

CHAPTER 06

CASE STUDIES

Real-Life Examples of How Integrating These Perspectives Has Helped Parents Manage Their Anger Effectively

Theory and strategies are essential in understanding how to manage anger effectively, but real-life examples can bring these concepts to life, showing how they work in practice. This chapter will present a series of case studies that illustrate how parents have successfully integrated the strategies discussed in previous chapters—such as cognitive-behavioral techniques, stress management, effective communication, and spiritual practices—into their daily lives to manage their anger and improve their relationships with their children.

Case Study 1: Cognitive-Behavioral Techniques in Action

Background:

Lisa, a single mother of two teenagers, found herself frequently losing her temper over what she perceived as her children's disrespectful behavior, particularly when they didn't follow household rules or complete their chores on time. Her anger often led to shouting matches, which only made the situation worse and strained her relationship with her children.

Challenges:

Lisa realized that her anger was not only damaging her relationship with her children but also causing her significant stress. She wanted to break the cycle of anger but didn't know where to start. Her goal was to improve her emotional control and find more effective ways to communicate her expectations to her children.

Strategy Implementation:

Lisa decided to try cognitive-behavioral techniques (CBT) after reading about their effectiveness in managing anger. She began by identifying her thought patterns that contributed to her anger, such as overgeneralizing ("My kids never listen to me") and personalizing ("They are doing this to disrespect me on purpose").

- Cognitive Restructuring: Lisa started practicing cognitive restructuring. When she noticed herself thinking, "They never listen," she challenged this thought by reminding herself of times when her children did follow the rules or were cooperative. She replaced her negative thoughts with more balanced ones, like, "They sometimes forget, but they do listen when I communicate clearly."

- Behavioral Activation: Recognizing that much of her anger stemmed from feeling overwhelmed by managing the household alone, Lisa incorporated more positive activities into her routine. She started exercising regularly, which helped her release pent-up frustration and approach her children with a calmer mindset.

- Problem-Solving: Lisa also implemented problem-solving techniques with her children. Instead of getting angry when chores weren't done, she sat down with them to discuss what was getting in the way and how they could all work together to ensure responsibilities were met.

Outcome:

Over time, Lisa noticed a significant reduction in her anger. By changing her thought patterns and involving her children in problem-solving, she not only managed her emotions better but also improved communication within the family. Her children responded positively to the changes, and the overall atmosphere at home became more cooperative and peaceful.

Case Study 2: Stress Management and Relaxation Techniques

Background:

John, a father of three young children, struggled with controlling his anger, particularly after long days at work. The stress of balancing a demanding job with parenting left him with little patience, and he found himself snapping at his children for minor infractions, like being too loud or not following instructions immediately.

Challenges:

John's primary challenge was managing the stress that seemed to fuel his anger. He recognized that his anger was often disproportionate to the situation, and he wanted to learn how to manage his stress better so that he could be more present and patient with his children.

Strategy Implementation:

John decided to focus on stress management techniques to help him regulate his emotions better and reduce his stress levels.

- Deep Breathing and Progressive Muscle Relaxation: John began practicing deep breathing exercises during his commute home from work. Before entering the house, he would sit in his car for a few minutes, focusing on his breath and releasing the tension in his body through progressive muscle relaxation. This practice helped him transition from work mode to home mode, leaving the stress of the day behind.

- Time Management: To reduce the stress of feeling overwhelmed, John implemented time management strategies. He started planning his day more effectively, setting realistic goals for work and home life, and delegating tasks where possible. This allowed him to manage his workload better and free up more time to spend with his family.

- Physical Activity: John incorporated regular physical activity into his routine. He found that jogging in the mornings not only helped him manage stress but also improved his mood throughout the day.

Outcome:

As John consistently practiced these stress management techniques, he noticed a significant decrease in his overall stress levels and, consequently, in his anger. He became more patient and less reactive with his children, leading to more positive interactions and a happier home environment. His ability to manage stress effectively allowed him to enjoy his time with his family more fully.

Case Study 3: Effective Communication and Conflict Resolution

Background:

Maria, a mother of a teenage daughter, often found herself in heated arguments with her daughter over issues like curfew, homework, and social media use. These arguments frequently escalated into yelling, leaving both Maria and her daughter feeling frustrated and disconnected.

Challenges:

Maria struggled with maintaining calm during conflicts and often felt that her daughter wasn't listening to her concerns. She wanted to find a way to communicate more effectively with her daughter and resolve conflicts without damaging their relationship.

Strategy Implementation:

Maria decided to focus on improving her communication skills and learning better conflict resolution techniques.

- Active Listening and "I" Statements: Maria made a conscious effort to practice active listening when talking to her daughter. She started by giving her full attention, reflecting back what she heard, and validating her daughter's feelings. Additionally, Maria replaced accusatory language with "I" statements, such as, "I feel worried when you stay out late because I care about your safety."

- Setting Clear Expectations: Maria and her daughter sat down to discuss expectations around curfew and social media use. They worked together to establish clear boundaries that both of them agreed on, which helped reduce misunderstandings and conflicts.

- Problem-Solving Together: When conflicts arose, Maria encouraged her daughter to participate in finding solutions. Instead of dictating rules, they brainstormed together on how to balance freedom with responsibility, which helped Maria's daughter feel more respected and involved in the decision-making process.

Outcome:

Maria's efforts to improve communication transformed her relationship with her daughter. Arguments became less frequent and less intense, and they were able to resolve conflicts more constructively. By fostering an environment of open dialogue and mutual respect, Maria and her daughter developed a stronger bond and a more harmonious relationship.

Case Study 4: Integrating Spiritual Practices for Emotional Balance

Background:

James, a father of two, had always been quick to anger, especially when things didn't go as planned. This tendency strained his relationship with his wife and children, as they often felt they were walking on eggshells around him. James was a man of faith and wanted to align his actions more closely with his spiritual beliefs, particularly in managing his anger.

Challenges:

James's challenge was to integrate his spiritual beliefs into his daily life in a way that would help him manage his anger and become a more patient and loving father and husband.

Strategy Implementation:

James decided to incorporate spiritual practices into his routine to help him cultivate greater emotional balance and reduce his anger.

- Daily Prayer and Reflection: James began starting each day with prayer, asking for guidance in managing his emotions and for the strength to respond to challenges with patience. He also included a brief reflection period in the evenings to assess how he handled his emotions during the day and to seek forgiveness for any lapses in temper.

- Mindfulness Meditation: In addition to prayer, James practiced mindfulness meditation, focusing on being present in the moment and accepting his feelings without judgment. This helped him become more aware of his triggers and more intentional in his responses.

- Forgiveness and Letting Go: James made a conscious effort to practice forgiveness, both toward himself when he lost his temper and toward others. He reflected on the spiritual teachings of forgiveness, using them as a guide to release any lingering anger or resentment.

Outcome:

Over time, James noticed a profound change in his emotional state. He became more patient and less reactive, and his family noticed the difference as well. The spiritual practices not only helped him manage his anger but also deepened his sense of peace and connection with his faith. His relationship with his wife and children improved as he became more present, understanding, and forgiving.

Case Study 5: Blending Multiple Strategies for Comprehensive Anger Management

Background:

Samantha, a working mother of a 5-year-old son, found herself struggling to balance the demands of her job and parenting. The stress of her daily responsibilities often led to irritability and anger, which she would sometimes take out on her son in the form of impatience and harsh words. Samantha was determined to find a way to manage her anger better for the sake of her son's emotional well-being.

Challenges:

Samantha's challenge was to address both the external stressors contributing to her anger and her internal emotional responses. She wanted to be a more patient and understanding parent, despite the pressures of her daily life.

Strategy Implementation:

Samantha decided to adopt a comprehensive approach, blending cognitive-behavioral techniques, stress management, effective communication, and spiritual practices.

- Cognitive Restructuring: Samantha worked on identifying and challenging the negative thoughts that fueled her anger, such as "I'm a bad mother because I can't do it all." She replaced these thoughts with more compassionate ones, like "I'm doing my best, and it's okay to ask for help."

- Relaxation Techniques: To manage her stress, Samantha practiced deep breathing exercises throughout the day, especially before interacting with her son after a long day at work. She also made time for short walks during lunch breaks to clear her mind and reduce stress.

- Effective Communication:

Samantha focused on improving her communication with her son, using clear and gentle language to set expectations and address any misbehavior. She also practiced active listening, making sure her son felt heard and understood.

- Spiritual Practices: Samantha incorporated daily prayer into her routine, asking for patience and wisdom in her parenting. She also practiced gratitude, reflecting on the positive aspects of her life and her relationship with her son.

Outcome:

The combination of these strategies had a transformative effect on Samantha's ability to manage her anger. She became more patient, both with herself and her son, and was better equipped to handle the stresses of her daily life without letting them negatively impact her parenting. Her son responded positively to the changes, and their relationship grew stronger as a result. Samantha's comprehensive approach to anger management allowed her to create a more peaceful and nurturing home environment.

These case studies demonstrate the effectiveness of integrating various strategies for managing anger in the context of parenting. Whether through cognitive-behavioral techniques, stress management, effective communication, or spiritual practices, each parent was able to find tools that worked for them, leading to significant improvements in their emotional control and relationships with their children.

The key takeaway from these examples is that managing anger is a multifaceted process that requires commitment, self-awareness, and a willingness to try different approaches until you find what works best for you. By applying the strategies discussed in this book, you too can develop the skills needed to manage your anger effectively and build stronger, more positive relationships with your children.

PRACTICAL APPLIACTIONS FOR PARENTS

Daily Routines: Incorporating Anger Management Strategies into Daily Parenting Routines

Successfully managing anger as a parent is not only about knowing the right strategies but also about integrating these strategies into your daily routines. By making anger management a consistent part of your daily life, you can create a more peaceful, balanced, and supportive environment for both yourself and your children. This chapter will guide you through practical ways to incorporate anger management techniques into your daily parenting routines, helping you to stay calm, focused, and connected with your children even in challenging situations.

1. Morning Routine: Setting a Positive Tone for the Day

The way you start your day can significantly influence your mood and how you handle stress and anger throughout the day. Establishing a morning routine that includes practices to promote calmness and mindfulness can help you approach the day with greater patience and emotional balance.

A. Morning Mindfulness or Meditation

Begin your day with a few minutes of mindfulness or meditation. This practice helps you center yourself, clear your mind, and set a positive intention for the day ahead.

- How to Practice Morning Mindfulness:

- Find a Quiet Space: Before your children wake up, find a quiet spot in your home where you can sit comfortably.

- Focus on Your Breath: Close your eyes and take several deep breaths, focusing on the sensation of the breath entering and leaving your body.

- Set an Intention: As you continue to breathe deeply, set an intention for your day. This could be something like, "Today, I will approach my children with patience and understanding."

- Practice for 5-10 Minutes: Spend 5-10 minutes in this state of mindfulness, allowing yourself to feel calm and centered before beginning your day.

B. Positive Affirmations

Incorporating positive affirmations into your morning routine can help reinforce a calm and confident mindset. Affirmations are positive statements that you repeat to yourself to promote self-empowerment and focus.

- Examples of Positive Affirmations:

- "I am a patient and loving parent."

- "I have the ability to handle challenges calmly and wisely."

- "Today, I will choose peace over anger."

- How to Use Affirmations:

- Repeat Daily: Repeat your chosen affirmations each morning, either silently or out loud. You can do this while getting ready for the day, during your morning meditation, or even while preparing breakfast.

- Personalize Them: Tailor your affirmations to reflect your specific goals and challenges. For example, if you struggle with impatience, you might use the affirmation, "I remain calm and patient even in difficult situations."

C. Morning Exercise

Physical activity is a powerful tool for managing stress and anger. Incorporating exercise into your morning routine can help release tension, boost your mood, and provide you with the energy you need to handle the day's challenges.

- How to Incorporate Morning Exercise:

- Choose an Activity You Enjoy: Whether it's a brisk walk, yoga, or a quick workout at home, choose an activity that you enjoy and that fits your schedule.

- Make it a Habit: Aim to exercise for at least 20-30 minutes each morning. This can be done before your children wake up or as part of your family's morning routine.

- Involve Your Children: If possible, involve your children in your morning exercise. This not only models healthy habits but also provides a bonding opportunity.

2. Midday Routine: Staying Grounded During the Day

The middle of the day can be a particularly stressful time, especially if you're juggling work, household responsibilities, and parenting. Incorporating anger management strategies into your midday routine can help you stay grounded and prevent stress from escalating into anger.

A. Mindful Breaks

Taking mindful breaks throughout the day can help you recharge and maintain emotional balance. These breaks don't have to be long; even a few minutes can make a significant difference.

- How to Take Mindful Breaks:

- Set a Timer: Set a timer on your phone or computer to remind you to take a short break every couple of hours.

- Practice Deep Breathing: During your break, practice deep breathing for 2-3 minutes. Focus on each breath, allowing your body to relax with each exhale.

- Do a Quick Body Scan: Close your eyes and mentally scan your body from head to toe, noticing any areas of tension. As you identify tension, consciously release it and relax those muscles.

B. Lunchtime Reflection

Use your lunch break as an opportunity to reflect on how your day is going and how you've managed your emotions so far. This reflection can help you make adjustments if needed and approach the rest of the day with renewed focus.

- How to Reflect at Lunchtime:

- Find a Quiet Spot: If possible, take your lunch in a quiet space where you can reflect without distractions.

- Ask Yourself Key Questions: Consider questions like, "How have I handled stress and anger today?" "What has gone well?" and "What could I do differently this afternoon?"

- Set a Midday Intention: Based on your reflection, set a new intention for the rest of the day. For example, "This afternoon, I will take deep breaths before responding to any stressful situations."

C. Healthy Eating for Emotional Balance

What you eat during the day can impact your mood and energy levels. Eating a balanced lunch that includes whole foods, lean proteins, and plenty of fruits and vegetables can help stabilize your blood sugar and prevent irritability.

- Tips for a Healthy Midday Meal:

- Include Whole Grains: Whole grains like brown rice, quinoa, or whole wheat bread provide sustained energy without the sugar crashes that can lead to irritability.

- Add Lean Protein: Lean proteins such as chicken, turkey, tofu, or legumes help maintain energy and focus throughout the day.

- Incorporate Fruits and Vegetables: Fresh fruits and vegetables provide essential vitamins and minerals that support mood regulation and overall well-being.

3. Afternoon and Evening Routine: Managing the After-School and Evening Transition

Afternoons and evenings, especially the transition from school or work to home life, can be a time of heightened stress and potential anger triggers. Establishing a routine that includes calming activities and effective communication can help manage this transition smoothly.

A. The After-School Transition

When children return home from school, they often bring with them their own stress and emotions from the day.

Creating a calm and structured after-school routine can help ease this transition and reduce the likelihood of conflict.

- Create a Calm Environment: Encourage a quiet and calm environment when your children come home. This might involve turning off the TV, putting away electronic devices, and spending a few minutes talking about each other's day.

- Snack and Relaxation Time: Offer a healthy snack and allow your children some time to relax before starting on homework or chores. This gives them a chance to unwind and transition from school mode to home mode.

- Check-In with Your Children: Take a few minutes to check in with your children about their day. Use active listening techniques to understand how they're feeling and address any concerns they might have.

B. Preparing for the Evening Routine

As you prepare for the evening, incorporating relaxation techniques and effective communication can help prevent stress and anger from building up.

- Prepare Dinner Together: If possible, involve your children in preparing dinner. This can be a calming and bonding activity that encourages communication and cooperation.

- Practice Deep Breathing Before Dinner: Before sitting down for dinner, take a few deep breaths as a family. This helps everyone transition from the busyness of the day to a more relaxed state, making mealtime more enjoyable.

C. Evening Wind-Down

The evening wind-down routine is crucial for setting a peaceful tone before bedtime. This routine should include activities that promote relaxation and emotional connection.

- Family Reflection Time: Spend a few minutes as a family reflecting on the day. Discuss what went well, share something you're grateful for, and talk about any challenges in a supportive way.

- Gratitude Practice: Encourage each family member to share one thing they're grateful for that day. This practice shifts the focus from stress to appreciation, helping to end the day on a positive note.

- Reading or Quiet Time: Incorporate a reading or quiet time before bed. This can be a calming way to end the day, helping both you and your children relax and prepare for sleep.

- Bedtime Affirmations: End the day with positive affirmations or a prayer, reinforcing a sense of peace and emotional balance. For example, "I am proud of how I handled today, and I look forward to tomorrow with a calm and open heart."

4. Handling Unexpected Stress and Anger Triggers

Despite your best efforts to maintain a calm routine, unexpected stressors and anger triggers are inevitable. Having a plan for handling these situations can help you stay grounded and respond constructively.

A. Pause and Breathe

When faced with an unexpected stressor or anger trigger, your first response should be to pause and breathe. This simple act can prevent an immediate reaction and give you the space to choose a more thoughtful response.

- How to Pause and Breathe:

- Take a Deep Breath: As soon as you feel anger rising, take a slow, deep breath. Inhale deeply through your nose, hold for a moment, and then exhale slowly through your mouth.

- Count to Ten: If needed, count to ten slowly as you breathe. This gives you a few extra seconds to calm down and think before responding.

- Consider Your Response: Ask yourself, "What's the best way to respond to this situation?" Choose a response that aligns with your values and goals, rather than reacting out of anger.

B. Use "I" Statements to Communicate

When addressing the situation, use "I" statements to express your feelings without blaming or criticizing others. This approach can help de-escalate the situation and lead to a more productive conversation.

- Example of an "I" Statement:

- "I feel frustrated when things don't go as planned because it makes it harder to stay on track. Can we work together to figure out a solution?"

C. Take a Break if Needed

If you find yourself overwhelmed by anger, it's okay to take a break before addressing the situation. This break can help you cool down and approach the problem with a clearer mind.

- How to Take a Break:

- Communicate the Need: Let others know that you need a few minutes to yourself. For example, "I need to step away for a moment to calm down. I'll be back shortly, and then we can talk."

- Engage in a Calming Activity: Use this break to engage in a calming activity, such as taking a walk, practicing deep breathing, or doing a quick mindfulness exercise.

- Return with a Plan: After your break, return to the situation with a plan for how to address the issue constructively.

5. Long-Term Strategies for Consistent Anger Management

In addition to daily routines, there are long-term strategies that can help you maintain consistent anger management over time. These strategies focus on ongoing self-reflection, personal growth, and building a supportive environment.

A. Regular Self-Reflection

Make self-reflection a regular part of your routine. This practice helps you stay aware of your emotional state, recognize patterns in your behavior, and make adjustments as needed.

- How to Practice Self-Reflection:

- Weekly Reflection: Set aside time each week to reflect on your emotional responses and how you managed stress and anger. Consider what worked well and what could be improved.

- Journaling: Keep a journal to record your thoughts, feelings, and experiences related to anger management. This can provide valuable insights and track your progress over time.

B. Seeking Support

Building a support network is crucial for long-term anger management. Whether it's through friends, family, or professional help, having people to turn to can make a significant difference.

- How to Build a Support Network:

- Stay Connected: Maintain regular contact with friends and family members who can offer emotional support and advice.

- Seek Professional Help: If you find that managing anger is particularly challenging, consider seeking help from a therapist or counselor who specializes in anger management.

- Join a Support Group: Consider joining a support group where you can share experiences and learn from others who are also working on managing their anger.

C. Continuous Learning and Growth

Anger management is an ongoing process that requires continuous learning and growth. Stay committed to improving your skills and expanding your knowledge over time.

- How to Continue Learning:

- Read Books and Articles: Continue reading books, articles, and other resources on anger management and emotional regulation.

- Attend Workshops or Classes: Consider attending workshops or classes on anger management, communication, or stress reduction.

- Practice New Techniques: Be open to trying new techniques and strategies as you learn more about anger management. Experiment with different approaches to find what works best for you.

Incorporating anger management strategies into your daily parenting routines is essential for creating a peaceful and balanced home environment. By establishing morning, midday, and evening routines that promote calmness, mindfulness, and effective communication, you can prevent stress and anger from building up and ensure that you approach your parenting responsibilities with patience and understanding.

Remember that anger management is not just about avoiding anger; it's about developing the skills to recognize, process, and respond to your emotions in a healthy way. By consistently practicing these strategies and making them a part of your daily life, you can build a stronger, more positive relationship with your children and create a home filled with love, respect, and emotional well-being.

As you continue to integrate these strategies into your routines, be patient with yourself and celebrate your progress. Anger management is a journey, and each step you take brings you closer to becoming the calm, confident, and compassionate parent you aspire to be.

Family Activities

Activities and Practices That Promote Emotional Health and Reduce Anger in the Family Setting

The family setting is a powerful environment for shaping emotional health and fostering positive relationships. Engaging in activities that promote emotional well-being can help reduce anger, strengthen family bonds, and create a supportive and loving home atmosphere. This chapter explores a variety of family activities and practices designed to enhance emotional health, improve communication, and reduce anger within the family.

1. The Importance of Family Activities for Emotional Health

Family activities play a crucial role in building strong emotional connections among family members. They provide opportunities for communication, shared experiences, and the development of trust and empathy. Regularly engaging in positive activities as a family can help prevent the build-up of stress and anger, promote mutual understanding, and create lasting memories that reinforce the family bond.

A. Strengthening Family Bonds

Engaging in regular family activities helps to create a sense of unity and belonging. These activities provide a shared space where family members can relax, have fun, and connect with one another without the pressures of daily responsibilities.

B. Developing Emotional Resilience

Family activities can help build emotional resilience by providing a safe environment for expressing feelings, practicing problem-solving, and learning how to manage stress together. This resilience is crucial in preventing anger from taking root and escalating within the family.

C. Encouraging Open Communication

Participating in activities together encourages open communication. Whether it's through playing games, cooking, or going on outings, these shared experiences provide natural opportunities for conversation, allowing family members to express themselves and listen to each other in a relaxed setting.

2. Family Activities to Promote Emotional Health and Reduce Anger

Incorporating specific activities into your family's routine can significantly enhance emotional health and reduce anger. The following activities are designed to be fun, engaging, and conducive to building strong, positive relationships.

A. Family Game Nights

Family game nights are an excellent way to promote teamwork, communication, and laughter—all of which are essential for emotional health. Playing games together allows family members to enjoy each other's company, practice good sportsmanship, and develop problem-solving skills in a low-pressure environment.

- Choosing the Right Games:

- Cooperative Games: Choose games that require teamwork rather than competition. Games where family members must work together to achieve a common goal can help build trust and cooperation.

- Board Games and Card Games: Classic board games and card games are great for family bonding. Choose games that are age-appropriate and that everyone can enjoy.

- Trivia or Quiz Games: Trivia games can be both educational and fun, encouraging family members to learn new things while enjoying some friendly competition.

- Setting the Mood:

- Create a Relaxed Atmosphere: Set up a comfortable space for game night, free from distractions. Provide snacks and drinks to keep everyone energized and engaged.

- Encourage Positive Interaction: Focus on the fun rather than on winning. Encourage family members to support each other, laugh at mistakes, and celebrate each other's successes.

- Benefits of Family Game Nights:

- Improves Communication: Game nights provide an opportunity for family members to talk, share stories, and engage in light-hearted conversation.

- Reduces Stress: Playing games can be a great stress reliever, helping to take everyone's mind off daily worries and tensions.

- Builds Emotional Connection: Regular game nights help strengthen the emotional bonds between family members, creating a sense of closeness and unity.

B. Outdoor Activities and Nature Walks

Spending time outdoors as a family has numerous benefits for emotional health. Nature walks, hikes, and other outdoor activities provide a break from the usual routine, reduce stress, and offer an opportunity for meaningful conversations in a relaxed setting.

- Ideas for Outdoor Activities:

- Nature Walks and Hikes: Explore local parks, nature reserves, or trails as a family. Use these walks as an opportunity to observe nature, talk about your day, or simply enjoy the peaceful surroundings.

- Picnics: Plan a family picnic in a nearby park. Bring along healthy snacks and spend time playing outdoor games, reading, or just relaxing together.

- Gardening: If you have a garden, involve the whole family in planting flowers, vegetables, or herbs. Gardening can be a therapeutic activity that fosters a sense of accomplishment and connection with nature.

- Benefits of Outdoor Activities:

- Reduces Stress: Being in nature has a calming effect, helping to reduce stress and anxiety while promoting relaxation and well-being.

- Encourages Physical Activity: Outdoor activities promote physical health, which is closely linked to emotional well-being. Regular exercise helps release endorphins, which boost mood and reduce the likelihood of anger.

- Fosters Connection: Spending time outdoors together encourages natural conversations and strengthens the family's emotional connection.

C. Family Meals and Cooking Together

Sharing meals as a family is a powerful way to connect emotionally and create a sense of belonging. Cooking together adds an extra layer of bonding, as it encourages teamwork, creativity, and shared responsibility.

- Incorporating Family Meals:

- Regular Family Dinners: Make it a habit to have dinner together as a family as often as possible. Use this time to talk about your day, share stories, and discuss any challenges or successes.

- Involve Everyone in Cooking: Assign different tasks in the kitchen to each family member, from chopping vegetables to setting the table. Cooking together can be a fun and educational experience for everyone involved.

- Theme Nights: Introduce theme nights where the family can cook dishes from different cultures or create new recipes together. This adds variety and excitement to mealtime.

- Benefits of Family Meals:

- Enhances Communication: Mealtime provides a natural setting for conversation, helping family members stay connected and aware of each other's lives.

- Promotes Healthy Eating: Family meals are an opportunity to teach children about healthy eating habits and to enjoy nutritious, homemade food together.

- Builds Teamwork: Cooking together requires cooperation and communication, helping to strengthen family bonds and reduce conflicts.

D. Family Mindfulness and Relaxation Practices

Practicing mindfulness and relaxation together as a family can help everyone manage stress, regulate emotions, and create a more peaceful home environment. These practices encourage presence, awareness, and calm, making them excellent tools for reducing anger and promoting emotional health.

- Mindfulness Activities for Families:

- Family Meditation: Set aside time each day or week for a short family meditation session. This can be as simple as sitting quietly together, focusing on your breath, and letting go of any tension or stress.

- Gratitude Practice: Encourage each family member to share something they are grateful for each day. This practice shifts the focus from stress and frustration to appreciation and positivity.

- Progressive Muscle Relaxation: Practice progressive muscle relaxation as a family, where you each take turns tensing and relaxing different muscle groups to release physical tension and promote relaxation.

- Incorporating Mindfulness into Daily Routines:

- Mindful Morning Routine: Start the day with a mindful activity, such as deep breathing, stretching, or setting a positive intention for the day as a family.

- Evening Wind-Down: End the day with a calming activity, such as reading a book together, listening to relaxing music, or practicing mindfulness before bedtime.

- Benefits of Mindfulness and Relaxation:

- Reduces Stress and Anger: Mindfulness helps family members become more aware of their emotions and reactions, making it easier to manage stress and prevent anger from escalating.

- Improves Focus and Presence: Regular mindfulness practice helps improve concentration and presence, allowing family members to be more attentive to each other.

- Creates a Calming Home Environment: Incorporating relaxation practices into the family routine promotes a sense of calm and tranquility, reducing overall stress levels in the home.

E. Creative Family Projects

Engaging in creative projects together as a family encourages self-expression, teamwork, and problem-solving. These projects can be both fun and therapeutic, helping to channel emotions in positive ways and fostering a sense of accomplishment.

- Ideas for Creative Family Projects:

- Art and Craft Projects: Set up a space for art and craft projects where family members can draw, paint, build, or create something together. This can be a great way to express emotions and bond over shared creativity.

- DIY Projects: Work on a DIY project together, such as building a birdhouse, decorating a room, or creating homemade gifts. These projects require cooperation and allow everyone to contribute their skills and ideas.

- Family Scrapbook: Create a family scrapbook where you can document memories, achievements, and special moments. This project helps reinforce positive experiences and serves as a reminder of the family's journey together.

- Benefits of Creative Projects:

- Enhances Emotional Expression: Creative projects provide a safe and constructive outlet for expressing emotions, reducing the likelihood of anger and frustration.

- Builds Teamwork and Problem-Solving Skills: Working together on a project encourages teamwork, communication, and problem-solving, all of which are essential for a harmonious family dynamic.

- Fosters a Sense of Accomplishment: Completing a creative project together gives family members a sense of achievement and pride, reinforcing positive behavior and collaboration.

3. Building Family Traditions

Family traditions are powerful tools for creating a sense of identity, continuity, and belonging. They provide structure and meaning to family life and can help anchor family members during times of stress or change.

A. Establishing Weekly or Monthly Traditions

Creating regular family traditions, whether weekly or monthly, helps build consistency and gives family members something to look forward to.

- Examples of Family Traditions:

- Weekly Movie Night: Choose a night each week for a family movie night. Take turns selecting the movie, and enjoy popcorn and snacks together.

- Monthly Outings: Plan a monthly family outing, such as a visit to a museum, a hike, or a day trip to a nearby city. These outings provide a change of scenery and an opportunity for family bonding.

- Family Meetings: Hold regular family meetings where everyone has a chance to discuss any issues, plan future activities, and share their thoughts and feelings. This practice encourages open communication and collaborative decision-making.

B. Celebrating Special Occasions

Celebrating special occasions, such as birthdays, holidays, and milestones, helps strengthen family bonds and create positive memories.

- Creating Meaningful Celebrations:

- Personalized Celebrations: Personalize celebrations to reflect your family's values, interests, and traditions. For example, if your family loves the outdoors, plan a nature-themed birthday party.

- Involving Everyone: Involve all family members in the planning and preparation for special occasions. This creates a sense of ownership and pride in the event.

- Focusing on Togetherness: Emphasize the importance of spending time together during special occasions, rather than focusing solely on gifts or material aspects.

- Benefits of Family Traditions:

- Strengthens Family Identity: Family traditions help create a shared identity and a sense of belonging, which is important for emotional stability and resilience.

- Provides Stability During Change: Traditions provide a sense of continuity and stability, which can be particularly comforting during times of change or stress.

- Creates Lasting Memories: Celebrating special occasions together helps create positive memories that reinforce the family's emotional bond.

4. Encouraging Ongoing Emotional Growth

In addition to regular activities, it's important to encourage ongoing emotional growth within the family. This involves creating an environment where emotional expression, self-awareness, and personal development are valued and supported.

A. Emotional Check-Ins

Regular emotional check-ins provide an opportunity for family members to share their feelings, discuss any concerns, and offer support to one another.

- How to Conduct Emotional Check-Ins:

- Set a Regular Time: Choose a regular time each day or week for emotional check-ins, such as during family meals or before bed.

- Ask Open-Ended Questions: Encourage family members to share their feelings by asking open-ended questions like, "How are you feeling today?" or "Is there anything on your mind that you'd like to talk about?"

- Listen and Validate: Listen actively to each person's response and validate their feelings. Offer support and encouragement as needed.

B. Encouraging Emotional Literacy

Teaching emotional literacy involves helping family members recognize, understand, and express their emotions in healthy ways.

- Ways to Encourage Emotional Literacy:

- Use Emotion Words: Incorporate emotion words into everyday conversations to help children and adults alike become more comfortable identifying and expressing their emotions.

- Read Books About Emotions: Choose books that explore different emotions and read them together as a family. Discuss the characters' feelings and how they handled different situations.

- Model Healthy Emotional Expression: Lead by example by expressing your own emotions in healthy ways. Show your children how to talk about their feelings and how to cope with difficult emotions.

C. Supporting Personal Growth and Self-Care

Encourage each family member to engage in activities that support their personal growth and well-being. This includes hobbies, self-care practices, and pursuing individual interests.

- Promoting Personal Growth:

- Support Hobbies and Interests: Encourage family members to pursue hobbies and interests that bring them joy and fulfillment. This promotes self-expression and emotional well-being.

- Teach Self-Care: Help your children develop self-care routines, such as regular exercise, healthy eating, and relaxation practices. Model self-care by prioritizing your own well-being as well.

- Benefits of Personal Growth:

- Enhances Emotional Health: Pursuing personal growth and self-care contributes to overall emotional health, making it easier to manage stress and prevent anger.

- Encourages Independence: Supporting individual interests helps family members develop independence and self-confidence, which are important for emotional resilience.

Family activities and practices are powerful tools for promoting emotional health and reducing anger in the family setting. By incorporating activities like family game nights, outdoor adventures, cooking together, mindfulness practices, and creative projects into your routine, you can create a positive and supportive home environment where everyone feels connected and valued.

Building family traditions, encouraging ongoing emotional growth, and supporting each other's personal development further strengthen the family bond and contribute to a harmonious and emotionally healthy household. Remember that the key to reducing anger and fostering emotional well-being lies in consistent, positive interactions and shared experiences that reinforce love, respect, and understanding.

As you integrate these activities into your family's routine, be patient and flexible, and focus on the joy of spending quality time together. By making emotional health a priority, you'll create a lasting foundation of peace, connection, and happiness for your family.

Role of Support Systems

Building a Support Network, Including Counseling and Support Groups, to Help Manage Anger

Managing anger effectively is often a multifaceted process that requires not only personal effort and strategies but also the support and guidance of others. Building a strong support network, which may include counseling, support groups, family, and friends, can provide the additional resources, encouragement, and accountability needed to successfully manage anger. This chapter explores the role of support systems in anger management and provides practical guidance on how to build and utilize these networks to foster emotional health and resilience.

1. The Importance of Support Systems in Anger Management

Support systems play a crucial role in managing anger by providing a safety net of emotional, social, and professional resources. These systems offer different perspectives, help individuals stay accountable to their goals, and provide emotional support during challenging times.

A. Emotional Support

A strong support network can provide the emotional backing needed to navigate difficult emotions, including anger. When individuals feel understood and supported, they are more likely to express their emotions in healthy ways and less likely to resort to anger as a means of coping.

- Emotional Validation: Friends, family, and counselors can validate your feelings, helping you feel seen and understood. This validation can reduce feelings of isolation and frustration, which are often underlying causes of anger.

- Safe Spaces: Support systems create safe environments where individuals can express their emotions without fear of judgment or retaliation. This safety is essential for working through anger constructively.

B. Accountability

Support systems help individuals stay accountable to their anger management goals. Whether through regular check-ins with a counselor or support group meetings, having others involved in your journey can motivate you to stay on track.

- Regular Feedback: Support systems can provide regular feedback on your progress, helping you identify areas of improvement and reinforcing positive changes.

- Encouragement: During setbacks or challenging times, a strong support network can offer encouragement and remind you of the progress you've made, helping you stay committed to your anger management plan.

C. Access to Resources and Expertise

Counselors, therapists, and support groups offer access to specialized knowledge and resources that can enhance your anger management efforts. These professionals can provide tools, techniques, and strategies tailored to your specific needs.

- Professional Guidance: Counselors and therapists bring expertise in emotional regulation, cognitive-behavioral techniques, and other therapeutic approaches that can be highly effective in managing anger.

- Peer Support: Support groups offer the experience and insights of others who are also working on managing their anger. This peer support can be invaluable in learning new strategies and gaining different perspectives.

2. Building a Support Network for Anger Management

Creating a robust support network involves identifying and engaging with individuals and resources that can provide the necessary emotional, social, and professional support. This network can include family, friends, counselors, support groups, and other community resources.

A. Involving Family and Friends

Family and friends are often the first line of support in managing anger. Their understanding, encouragement, and involvement can significantly impact your ability to control your emotions and stay committed to your anger management goals.

- Communicating Your Needs: It's important to communicate openly with your family and friends about your anger management goals and how they can support you. Let them know what triggers your anger, what you're working on, and how they can help, whether by offering a listening ear, providing feedback, or simply being patient during difficult times.

- Setting Boundaries: While involving loved ones is crucial, it's also important to set healthy boundaries to prevent them from feeling overwhelmed or burdened by your anger management journey. Ensure that your relationships remain balanced, where both parties' needs are respected.

- Engaging in Shared Activities: Participating in activities that promote emotional health, such as exercise, mindfulness practices, or creative projects, can strengthen your bond with loved ones and provide mutual support in managing stress and anger.

B. Seeking Professional Counseling

Counseling offers a structured and professional environment for addressing anger issues. A trained counselor or therapist can help you explore the root causes of your anger, develop effective coping strategies, and work through any underlying emotional issues that may be contributing to your anger.

- Types of Counseling for Anger Management:

- Individual Counseling: In one-on-one sessions, a counselor can work with you to identify the specific triggers and patterns that contribute to your anger. They can also help you develop personalized strategies for managing your emotions and improving your relationships.

- Cognitive-Behavioral Therapy (CBT): CBT is a common therapeutic approach for anger management. It focuses on identifying and changing negative thought patterns and behaviors that contribute to anger, replacing them with more constructive ways of thinking and acting.

- Family Counseling: If your anger significantly impacts your family relationships, family counseling can be beneficial. This type of counseling involves working with your family members to improve communication, resolve conflicts, and build a more supportive home environment.

- Finding a Counselor:

- Referrals: Ask your primary care doctor, friends, or family members for referrals to reputable counselors or therapists who specialize in anger management.

- Online Resources: Many online platforms provide directories of licensed counselors and therapists, allowing you to search for professionals based on their specialization, location, and patient reviews.

- Community Resources: Local community centers, mental health clinics, and religious organizations often offer counseling services at reduced rates or for free, making professional help more accessible.

C. Joining Support Groups

Support groups provide a community of individuals who are facing similar challenges in managing anger. These groups offer a space for sharing experiences, discussing strategies, and receiving encouragement from peers who understand what you're going through.

- Benefits of Support Groups:

- Shared Experiences: Hearing others' stories can provide comfort and reduce feelings of isolation. It can also offer new perspectives and strategies that you may not have considered.

- Accountability: Regularly attending support group meetings helps keep you accountable to your anger management goals and provides ongoing motivation to continue working on your emotional health.

- Emotional Support: Support groups offer a non-judgmental space where you can express your feelings, receive validation, and gain emotional support from others who are also working through similar issues.

- Finding Support Groups:

- Local Community Centers: Many community centers and mental health organizations host support groups for anger management. Check with local centers or online directories to find a group that meets your needs.

- Online Support Groups: If attending in-person meetings is difficult, consider joining an online support group. These groups often provide the same benefits as in-person groups, with the added convenience of participating from home.

- Specialized Groups: Some support groups are tailored to specific populations, such as parents, men, women, or those dealing with specific types of anger (e.g., anger related to trauma). Finding a group that aligns with your experiences can enhance the support you receive.

D. Utilizing Online Resources and Apps

In addition to in-person support, there are numerous online resources and apps designed to help individuals manage anger. These tools can supplement your support network by providing additional guidance, strategies, and support.

- Online Counseling Services: Platforms like BetterHelp and Talkspace offer online counseling with licensed therapists, making it easier to access professional support from anywhere.

- Anger Management Apps: Apps such as "Anger Management" and "Calm" offer tools for tracking your emotions, practicing relaxation techniques, and learning new strategies for managing anger. These apps often include guided exercises, mood tracking, and reminders to help you stay on track.

- Educational Websites and Blogs: Websites like the American Psychological Association (APA) and Mayo Clinic provide educational resources on anger management, including articles, videos, and self-help tools.

3. Engaging with Community Resources

Community resources can play a significant role in building a support network for anger management. These resources often provide additional services, such as educational workshops, peer mentoring, and group activities that promote emotional health.

A. Community Centers and Non-Profit Organizations

Community centers and non-profit organizations often offer programs and services focused on mental health, including anger management workshops, support groups, and counseling services.

- Workshops and Seminars: Look for workshops and seminars on anger management, emotional regulation, and stress reduction. These programs are often led by professionals and can provide valuable insights and tools for managing anger.

- Peer Mentoring: Some organizations offer peer mentoring programs, where individuals can receive one-on-one support from someone who has successfully managed their own anger issues. This mentorship can provide guidance, encouragement, and a sense of accountability.

B. Religious and Spiritual Communities

For many individuals, religious and spiritual communities offer a vital source of support in managing anger. These communities often provide not only emotional and social support but also spiritual guidance that can help in dealing with anger.

- Counseling and Support Groups: Many religious organizations offer counseling services and support groups for anger management. These programs often incorporate spiritual practices, such as prayer, meditation, and reflection, which can be powerful tools in managing anger.

- Spiritual Guidance: Spiritual leaders, such as pastors, rabbis, or imams, can provide guidance and support in managing anger from a spiritual perspective. They can offer teachings, scriptures, and practices that align with your beliefs and help you find peace and balance.

- Community Support: Being part of a religious or spiritual community provides a sense of belonging and support. Regular participation in community events, services, and activities can foster emotional health and provide a network of individuals who care about your well-being.

C. Educational Institutions and Programs

Educational institutions, such as universities and community colleges, often offer courses, workshops, and counseling services that can support anger management efforts.

- Counseling Services: Many educational institutions offer free or low-cost counseling services to students, staff, and sometimes the general public. These services can include individual counseling, group therapy, and anger management workshops.

- Continuing Education Courses: Consider enrolling in continuing education courses focused on psychology, emotional regulation, or stress management. These courses can provide a deeper understanding of anger and equip you with new strategies for managing it.

4. Maintaining and Nurturing Your Support Network

Building a support network is only the first step; maintaining and nurturing these relationships is equally important for long-term success in managing anger. Regularly engaging with your support system, showing appreciation, and contributing to the support of others are key to keeping these connections strong.

A. Regular Communication and Check-Ins

Maintain regular communication with your support network, whether through phone calls, texts, emails, or in-person meetings. Regular check-ins help keep relationships strong and provide ongoing opportunities for support and feedback.

- Set Regular Meetings: Schedule regular check-ins with your counselor, support group, or close friends to discuss your progress, challenges, and any new strategies you're trying.

- Be Open and Honest: During these check-ins, be open and honest about your experiences, both positive and negative. This transparency helps build trust and allows your support network to provide more meaningful feedback and support.

B. Showing Appreciation and Gratitude

Expressing appreciation and gratitude to those in your support network reinforces these relationships and encourages ongoing support. Recognize the contributions of others and let them know how much their support means to you.

- Thank You Notes: Send a thank you note or message to your counselor, support group leader, or friends who have been particularly supportive. Let them know how their help has impacted your journey.

- Reciprocal Support: Offer your support in return. Whether it's lending a listening ear, providing advice, or helping out in some other way, showing that you're there for others strengthens the mutual support within your network.

C. Staying Engaged and Involved

Stay actively engaged with your support network by participating in group activities, attending meetings, and staying connected with your counselor. The more involved you are, the more benefits you'll receive from these relationships.

- Attend Meetings Regularly: Make a commitment to attend support group meetings or counseling sessions regularly, even when you're feeling better. Consistent engagement helps maintain your progress and provides ongoing reinforcement of your anger management strategies.

- Contribute to the Group: In support groups, actively contribute by sharing your experiences, offering advice, and supporting others. This involvement not only helps others but also reinforces your own learning and growth.

Building and maintaining a strong support network is a vital component of successful anger management. Whether through family and friends, professional counseling, support groups, or community resources, these networks provide the emotional, social, and professional support needed to navigate the challenges of managing anger.

By surrounding yourself with supportive individuals and resources, you gain access to a wealth of knowledge, encouragement, and accountability that can help you stay on track and achieve your goals. Remember that managing anger is a journey that benefits greatly from the guidance and support of others. By actively engaging with your support network, showing appreciation, and staying committed to your growth, you can build a foundation of emotional health and resilience that will serve you and your loved ones for years to come.

As you continue to work on managing your anger, lean on your support network for strength, guidance, and encouragement. Together, you can overcome challenges, celebrate successes, and create a more peaceful and fulfilling life.

CHAPTER 08

TEACHING CHILDREN ABOUT ANGER

Modeling Behavior: How Parents Can Model Healthy Anger Management for Their Children

As parents, one of the most powerful tools you have in teaching your children about anger management is your own behavior. Children learn by observing the actions and reactions of those around them, particularly their parents. When you model healthy ways to manage anger, you not only teach your children how to handle their own emotions but also create a positive and supportive environment where emotional health is a priority. This chapter will explore how parents can effectively model healthy anger management behaviors for their children, helping them develop the skills they need to manage their emotions throughout their lives.

1. The Impact of Parental Modeling on Children's Emotional Development

Children are keen observers, and they often mimic the behaviors they see in their parents. This is especially true when it comes to emotional regulation and managing anger. By modeling healthy anger management, you provide your children with a blueprint for how to handle their own emotions in a constructive way.

A. Understanding the Role of Modeling

Modeling is a form of learning where children observe and imitate the behaviors of others. This type of learning is particularly powerful in the early years of a child's development but continues to influence behavior throughout adolescence and into adulthood.

- Direct Observation: Children watch how you react in various situations, particularly stressful or frustrating ones. If they see you managing your anger calmly and constructively, they are more likely to adopt similar behaviors.

- Indirect Learning: Even when you're not directly interacting with your child, they may still observe how you handle anger in interactions with others—whether it's a spouse, a friend, or a stranger. These observations shape their understanding of what is acceptable and effective behavior.

B. The Consequences of Unhealthy Anger Modeling

When parents model unhealthy anger management, such as yelling, blaming, or physical aggression, children may internalize these behaviors as acceptable ways to express anger. This can lead to a range of negative outcomes, including:

- Increased Aggression: Children who witness aggressive behavior may become more aggressive themselves, using similar tactics to express their own frustrations.

- Emotional Distress: Exposure to frequent, intense anger can cause children to feel anxious, fearful, or insecure, which can affect their emotional well-being and development.

- Impaired Relationships: Children who learn unhealthy anger management techniques may struggle with forming and maintaining healthy relationships, both during childhood and later in life.

C. The Benefits of Healthy Anger Modeling

On the other hand, when parents model healthy anger management, the benefits are substantial:

- Emotional Regulation: Children learn to regulate their own emotions, leading to better control over their reactions and a lower likelihood of anger escalating into aggression.

- Problem-Solving Skills: By observing parents who handle anger constructively, children learn to approach conflicts with a problem-solving mindset, focusing on finding solutions rather than assigning blame.

- Stronger Relationships: Children who learn healthy anger management are better equipped to build and maintain positive relationships, characterized by effective communication and mutual respect.

2. Key Strategies for Modeling Healthy Anger Management

To effectively model healthy anger management for your children, it's important to incorporate specific strategies into your daily behavior. These strategies demonstrate how to handle anger in a way that is both constructive and compassionate.

A. Practice Self-Awareness

Self-awareness is the foundation of healthy anger management. It involves recognizing your own emotions, understanding what triggers your anger, and being mindful of how your behavior impacts those around you.

- Recognize Your Triggers: Identify the situations or behaviors that tend to trigger your anger. By understanding your triggers, you can better anticipate and manage your emotional responses before they escalate.

- Monitor Your Reactions: Pay attention to how your body responds to anger. Physical signs like increased heart rate, muscle tension, or a change in tone of voice can signal that your anger is rising. Recognizing these signs early allows you to take steps to calm down before reacting.

- Reflect on Your Behavior: After an anger-provoking incident, take time to reflect on how you handled the situation. Consider what worked well, what didn't, and how you might approach similar situations in the future.

B. Demonstrate Calmness Under Pressure

One of the most powerful ways to model healthy anger management is to remain calm in the face of stress or frustration. This demonstrates to your children that it's possible to handle difficult emotions without losing control.

- Use Calm, Steady Voice: When you feel anger rising, make a conscious effort to speak in a calm and steady voice. This helps to de-escalate the situation and sets a positive example for your children.

- Take a Pause: If you're feeling overwhelmed by anger, take a moment to pause and collect your thoughts before responding. This pause can be as simple as taking a deep breath or counting to ten. Let your children see you taking this pause, so they understand that it's okay to take a moment to calm down before reacting.

- Engage in De-escalation Techniques: Model techniques like deep breathing, progressive muscle relaxation, or mindfulness to calm your body and mind. Explain to your children what you're doing and why, so they can learn to use these techniques themselves.

C. Use "I" Statements

"I" statements are a way of expressing your feelings without blaming or criticizing others. This approach helps to prevent defensiveness and promotes constructive communication.

- How to Use "I" Statements:

- Express Your Feelings: Start with "I feel..." to describe how you're feeling. For example, "I feel frustrated..."

- Describe the Behavior: Follow with a description of the behavior that's causing the feeling. For example, "...when the toys are left out after I asked for them to be put away."

- Explain the Impact: Explain the impact of the behavior on you or the situation. For example, "...because it makes it harder for me to keep the house clean."

- Suggest a Solution: End with a suggestion for how to address the issue. For example, "Let's work together to clean up the toys before dinner."

- Modeling "I" Statements: When you use "I" statements in front of your children, you teach them how to express their emotions in a way that is respectful and constructive. Over time, they will learn to use this technique to communicate their own feelings and resolve conflicts.

D. Show Empathy and Understanding

Empathy is the ability to understand and share the feelings of others. By modeling empathy, you teach your children the importance of considering other people's perspectives and responding to them with kindness and understanding.

- Acknowledge Your Child's Feelings: When your child is angry or upset, acknowledge their feelings without judgment. For example, "I see that you're really frustrated right now. It's okay to feel that way."

- Express Empathy: Show empathy by trying to understand what your child is experiencing. For example, "I know it's hard when things don't go the way you want them to. I've felt that way too."

- Respond with Compassion: When addressing your child's anger, respond with compassion rather than punishment. Offer support and guidance to help them work through their emotions constructively.

- Modeling Empathy: By consistently showing empathy in your interactions with your children and others, you model the importance of understanding and responding to emotions with care and kindness.

E. Resolve Conflicts Constructively

Conflicts are inevitable, but how you handle them sets the tone for how your children will approach conflicts in their own lives. Demonstrating constructive conflict resolution teaches your children to approach disagreements with a focus on solutions rather than blame.

- Stay Focused on the Issue: When resolving a conflict, focus on the specific issue at hand rather than bringing up past grievances. This helps to keep the conversation productive and prevents it from escalating.

- Collaborate on Solutions: Involve your children in finding solutions to conflicts. This teaches them problem-solving skills and reinforces the idea that conflicts can be resolved through cooperation rather than confrontation.

- Apologize When Necessary: If you lose your temper or make a mistake, be willing to apologize to your children. This demonstrates accountability and shows that everyone, including parents, can learn from their mistakes.

- Modeling Conflict Resolution: When your children see you resolving conflicts calmly and constructively, they learn that disagreements don't have to be destructive and that it's possible to work through differences in a respectful manner.

F. Practice Forgiveness

Forgiveness is a critical component of healthy anger management. It involves letting go of resentment and moving forward without holding grudges. By modeling forgiveness, you teach your children the value of healing and maintaining positive relationships.

- Forgive Yourself: Show your children that it's okay to make mistakes and that self-forgiveness is an important part of growth. If you lose your temper, acknowledge it, and forgive yourself as you work to improve.

- Forgive Others: Demonstrate forgiveness in your interactions with others, whether it's your partner, friends, or strangers. Let your children see you letting go of anger and resentment in favor of understanding and reconciliation.

- Discuss Forgiveness: Talk to your children about the importance of forgiveness and how it helps to heal relationships and prevent anger from taking root.

- Modeling Forgiveness: When you model forgiveness, you help your children understand that holding onto anger is harmful and that letting go is a healthier and more positive approach to relationships.

3. Incorporating Healthy Anger Management into Daily Family Life

In addition to modeling healthy anger management behaviors, it's important to incorporate practices into your daily family life that reinforce these lessons. These practices help create a home environment where emotional health is prioritized and where children feel supported in managing their own anger.

A. Establishing Family Rules Around Anger

Setting clear family rules around how anger is expressed and managed helps to create consistency and reinforces the behaviors you're modeling.

- Examples of Family Rules:

- No Yelling: Encourage family members to use calm voices, even when they're upset. This rule helps to prevent anger from escalating and teaches children to express their feelings without raising their voices.

- Take a Break: If someone feels overwhelmed by anger, it's okay to take a break and return to the conversation when they've calmed down. This rule reinforces the importance of managing emotions before responding.

- Respectful Communication: All family members should speak to each other with respect, even during disagreements. This rule ensures that conflicts are handled constructively and that everyone's feelings are considered.

B. Encouraging Open Communication

Create an environment where open communication is encouraged, and where children feel safe expressing their emotions.

- Regular Check-Ins: Schedule regular family check-ins where everyone has a chance to share their feelings and discuss any issues. These check-ins provide an opportunity to address concerns before they escalate into anger.

- Open-Door Policy: Let your children know that they can come to you at any time to talk about their feelings, including anger. This open-door policy helps to build trust and encourages children to seek support when needed.

C. Practicing Mindfulness Together

Mindfulness practices can help the entire family manage stress and anger by promoting awareness, presence, and emotional regulation.

- Family Mindfulness Sessions: Set aside time each day or week for family mindfulness sessions. These sessions can include deep breathing, guided meditation, or simply sitting quietly together and focusing on the present moment.

- Mindful Mornings: Start the day with a mindful activity, such as stretching, deep breathing, or setting an intention for the day. This practice helps everyone begin the day with a calm and focused mindset.

D. Reinforcing Positive Behavior

When your children demonstrate healthy anger management behaviors, reinforce these actions with praise and encouragement. Positive reinforcement helps to solidify these behaviors and encourages your children to continue practicing them.

- Specific Praise: When praising your child, be specific about what they did well. For example, "I'm proud of how you stayed calm and explained how you were feeling instead of yelling."

- Encouragement: Offer encouragement when your child is working on managing their anger. Let them know that it's okay to struggle and that you're proud of the effort they're putting in.

E. Leading by Example in All Situations

Remember that your children are always watching and learning from your behavior. Whether you're at home, in public, or interacting with others, strive to lead by example by consistently modeling healthy anger management.

- Public Behavior: Be mindful of how you handle anger in public settings, such as during interactions with customer service representatives, other drivers, or strangers. Your children will observe how you manage these situations and will take cues from your behavior.

- Interactions with Your Partner: Your relationship with your partner is another area where modeling is crucial. Show your children how to handle disagreements with respect, empathy, and a focus on resolution.

4. Addressing Challenges in Modeling Healthy Anger Management

Modeling healthy anger management isn't always easy, and there will be times when you fall short of your goals. It's important to acknowledge these challenges, learn from them, and continue working towards improvement.

A. Acknowledging Mistakes

Everyone makes mistakes, and it's important to acknowledge them rather than pretending they didn't happen. When you acknowledge your mistakes, you show your children that it's okay to be imperfect and that growth is a continuous process.

- Apologize: If you lose your temper or handle a situation poorly, apologize to your children. Let them know that you recognize your mistake and that you're committed to doing better in the future.

- Discuss What Happened: Use the situation as a learning opportunity. Discuss what triggered your anger, how you reacted, and what you could do differently next time.

B. Seeking Support

If you're struggling to model healthy anger management, don't hesitate to seek support. Whether through counseling, support groups, or talking with a trusted friend, getting help can provide you with the tools and encouragement you need to improve.

- Counseling: Consider working with a counselor to explore your anger triggers and develop strategies for managing your emotions more effectively. A counselor can provide personalized guidance and support as you work on modeling healthy behavior for your children.

- Support Groups: Joining a support group for parents can offer a space to share experiences, gain insights, and receive encouragement from others who are also working on managing their anger.

C. Continuing to Learn and Grow

Anger management is an ongoing journey, and there's always room for improvement. Continue to learn new strategies, reflect on your behavior, and strive to model the best possible behavior for your children.

- Educational Resources: Keep learning about anger management through books, articles, workshops, and other resources. The more knowledge you have, the better equipped you'll be to model healthy behavior.

- Personal Reflection: Regularly reflect on your progress, celebrate your successes, and identify areas where you can continue to grow. Personal reflection helps to keep you focused on your goals and committed to your growth.

Modeling healthy anger management is one of the most powerful ways parents can teach their children how to handle emotions constructively. By practicing self-awareness, demonstrating calmness under pressure, using "I" statements, showing empathy, resolving conflicts constructively, and practicing forgiveness, you provide your children with a valuable blueprint for managing their own anger.

Incorporating these behaviors into your daily life, setting clear family rules, encouraging open communication, and practicing mindfulness together all contribute to a positive and supportive home environment. While challenges may arise, acknowledging your mistakes, seeking support, and committing to continuous growth will help you become the best possible role model for your children.

As you work on modeling healthy anger management, remember that your efforts have a lasting impact on your children's emotional development. By showing them how to handle anger with grace, compassion, and respect, you equip them with the tools they need to navigate their own emotions and build strong, positive relationships throughout their lives.

Teaching Skills

Strategies for Teaching Children to Understand and Manage Their Own Emotions

Helping children understand and manage their emotions is a crucial aspect of their development. By equipping them with the skills they need to navigate their feelings, parents can foster emotional resilience, self-regulation, and healthy relationships. This chapter will explore various strategies that parents can use to teach their children about emotions and provide practical tools for managing those emotions effectively.

1. The Importance of Emotional Intelligence in Children

Emotional intelligence (EI) refers to the ability to recognize, understand, and manage one's own emotions, as well as the ability to recognize and influence the emotions of others. Developing EI in children is essential for their overall well-being and success in life.

A. Benefits of Emotional Intelligence

- Improved Relationships: Children with high emotional intelligence are better able to form and maintain healthy relationships. They can empathize with others, communicate their feelings effectively, and navigate social situations with greater ease.

- Better Academic Performance: Emotional intelligence is linked to better academic performance. Children who can manage their emotions are more focused, less likely to be distracted by stress, and more capable of handling the challenges of schoolwork.

- Enhanced Mental Health: Children who understand and manage their emotions are less likely to experience anxiety, depression, or other emotional difficulties. They develop coping strategies that help them navigate life's ups and downs.

B. The Role of Parents in Developing Emotional Intelligence

Parents play a key role in nurturing their children's emotional intelligence. By teaching children to recognize and manage their emotions, parents can help them develop the skills needed to navigate the complexities of life with confidence and resilience.

- Modeling Behavior: Children learn by observing their parents. By modeling healthy emotional expression and regulation, parents provide a powerful example for their children to follow.

- Teaching Explicit Skills: Parents can teach their children specific skills for recognizing, understanding, and managing emotions. These skills form the foundation of emotional intelligence and set children up for success in all areas of life.

2. Strategies for Teaching Children About Emotions

Teaching children about emotions involves helping them recognize and label their feelings, understand what triggers those emotions, and develop healthy ways to express and manage them.

A. Helping Children Recognize and Label Their Emotions

The first step in teaching emotional intelligence is helping children recognize and label their emotions. This skill is crucial because it allows children to understand what they are feeling and why.

- Use Emotion Words Frequently: Incorporate emotion words into daily conversations. For example, instead of simply saying, "You're upset," you might say, "You seem frustrated because your toy isn't working." This helps children build a vocabulary for their emotions.

- Read Books About Emotions: Books that explore different emotions can be a valuable tool in teaching children about feelings. After reading, discuss the characters' emotions and ask your child how they might feel in a similar situation.

- Emotion Charts: Create or use an emotion chart that visually represents different emotions. Encourage your child to point to the emotion they're feeling at different times of the day. This can be particularly helpful for younger children who may struggle to articulate their feelings.

- Label Your Own Emotions: Model the behavior by labeling your own emotions. For example, "I'm feeling a bit stressed today because I have a lot of work to do, but I'm going to take some deep breaths to help me stay calm."

B. Teaching Emotional Awareness and Triggers

Understanding what triggers certain emotions is a critical component of emotional intelligence. Teaching children to identify these triggers helps them become more aware of their emotional responses and how to manage them.

- Discuss Triggers: Talk with your child about what triggers different emotions. For example, ask, "What makes you feel happy?" or "What usually makes you feel angry?" These discussions help children become more aware of the connection between events and their emotional responses.

- Use Examples from Daily Life: Use real-life situations to teach about emotional triggers. For instance, if your child is upset after losing a game, discuss how losing can trigger feelings of disappointment and what they can do to manage those feelings.

- Mindfulness Activities: Encourage mindfulness practices that help children become more aware of their emotional states and triggers. Simple mindfulness exercises, like focusing on their breathing or paying attention to how their body feels, can increase their emotional awareness.

C. Developing Healthy Emotional Expression

Teaching children how to express their emotions in healthy ways is essential for emotional regulation. Children need to know that all emotions are valid, but how they express those emotions matters.

- Encourage Open Communication: Create a safe space where your child feels comfortable expressing their emotions without fear of judgment. Let them know that it's okay to talk about their feelings and that you're there to listen.

- Role-Playing: Use role-playing to practice expressing emotions in different scenarios. For example, you can role-play a situation where your child is upset with a friend, and together you can explore different ways to express those feelings.

- Teach "I" Statements: Teach your child to use "I" statements to express their emotions. For example, "I feel sad when you don't want to play with me" is a constructive way for a child to express their feelings without blaming others.

- Validate Their Feelings: When your child expresses their emotions, validate their feelings by acknowledging them. For example, "I understand that you're feeling angry because you didn't get your way, and that's okay. Let's talk about it."

D. Equipping Children with Coping Strategies

Coping strategies are tools that help children manage their emotions, especially when they're feeling overwhelmed.

Teaching these strategies early on can help children develop resilience and self-regulation.

- Deep Breathing Exercises: Teach your child simple deep breathing exercises to calm down when they're upset. For younger children, you can make it fun by pretending to blow up a balloon or imagining they're blowing out candles on a birthday cake.

- Time-Out for Reflection: Instead of using time-out as a punishment, use it as a time for reflection. Encourage your child to take a break when they're feeling angry or frustrated, giving them time to calm down and think about how they want to respond.

- Positive Visualization: Teach your child to use positive visualization as a way to cope with negative emotions. For example, when they're feeling anxious, they can close their eyes and imagine themselves in a place where they feel safe and happy.

- Journaling: Encourage older children to keep a journal where they can write about their emotions and what triggers them. Journaling can be a powerful tool for processing emotions and reflecting on how they handle different situations.

- Physical Activity: Physical activity can be a great way for children to release pent-up energy and emotions.

Encourage your child to go for a run, jump on a trampoline, or engage in any other physical activity they enjoy when they're feeling overwhelmed.

E. Teaching Problem-Solving Skills

Problem-solving is a key component of emotional regulation. By teaching children how to solve problems, you empower them to manage situations that might otherwise lead to frustration or anger.

- Identify the Problem: Teach your child to identify the problem they're facing. For example, "The problem is that you're upset because your toy broke."

- Brainstorm Solutions: Encourage your child to think of different ways to solve the problem. Guide them in considering both the short-term and long-term consequences of each solution.

- Evaluate and Choose a Solution: Help your child evaluate the possible solutions and choose the one they think is best. This process teaches them to weigh options and make thoughtful decisions.

- Reflect on the Outcome: After trying a solution, discuss with your child how it worked out. This reflection helps them learn from their experiences and improve their problem-solving skills for the future.

F. Building Empathy and Understanding Others' Emotions

Empathy is the ability to understand and share the feelings of others. Teaching empathy is crucial for helping children develop strong social connections and navigate relationships effectively.

- Model Empathy: Show empathy in your daily interactions, both with your child and others. For example, "I see that your friend is upset. Let's think about how we can help them feel better."

- Discuss Different Perspectives: Encourage your child to consider how others might be feeling in different situations. For example, after reading a story or watching a movie, ask, "How do you think that character felt? Why do you think they acted that way?"

- Teach Active Listening: Teach your child to listen actively when others are speaking. This involves making eye contact, nodding, and responding thoughtfully. Active listening helps children understand others' emotions and respond with empathy.

- Practice Compassionate Responses: Encourage your child to respond to others with kindness and compassion, even when they disagree or feel upset. For example, if a sibling is upset, your child might offer comfort or help find a solution to the problem.

3. Creating a Supportive Environment for Emotional Learning

To effectively teach children about emotions, it's important to create a home environment that supports emotional learning and growth. This environment should be safe, nurturing, and open to communication.

A. Establishing a Safe and Open Environment

Children need to feel safe expressing their emotions without fear of punishment or ridicule. Establishing a safe and open environment encourages them to share their feelings and ask for help when needed.

- Encourage Open Dialogue: Regularly check in with your child about their feelings and experiences. Let them know that no emotion is wrong and that they can talk to you about anything.

- Avoid Punishing Emotional Expression: Instead of punishing your child for expressing emotions like anger or sadness, guide them in finding appropriate ways to express those feelings. For example, if they shout in frustration, encourage them to use words to explain what's bothering them instead.

- Be Patient and Understanding: Children may not always have the words to express their emotions or the ability to manage them effectively. Be patient as they learn, and offer guidance with empathy and understanding.

B. Encouraging Emotional Literacy in Daily Life

Incorporate emotional literacy into your daily routines and interactions. By making emotional learning a regular part of your child's life, you reinforce the importance of understanding and managing emotions.

- Emotion of the Day: Introduce an "emotion of the day" where you focus on a specific emotion, discussing what it feels like, what might trigger it, and how to manage it. This can be a fun way to build emotional vocabulary and understanding.

- Storytelling with Emotions: When reading stories or watching movies, discuss the emotions of the characters and how they handled different situations. Ask your child what they might have done differently and why.

- Emotional Check-Ins: Regularly ask your child how they're feeling throughout the day. These check-ins help your child become more aware of their emotions and encourage open communication.

C. Reinforcing Positive Emotional Behaviors

When your child demonstrates healthy emotional behaviors, reinforce these actions with praise and encouragement. Positive reinforcement helps children understand the value of emotional regulation and encourages them to continue practicing these skills.

- Specific Praise: Praise your child specifically for their emotional behavior. For example, "I'm really proud of how you stayed calm and explained how you were feeling when you were upset."

- Encouragement: Offer encouragement when your child is working on managing their emotions. Let them know that it's okay to struggle and that you're proud of their efforts to improve.

- Celebrate Progress: Celebrate milestones in your child's emotional development, such as successfully managing a difficult emotion or using a new coping strategy. These celebrations reinforce the importance of emotional growth.

D. Leading by Example

As a parent, your behavior is a powerful model for your child. By consistently demonstrating healthy emotional regulation, you provide a living example of how to manage emotions effectively.

- Manage Your Own Emotions: Show your child how you manage your own emotions, whether it's taking deep breaths when you're frustrated or expressing your feelings calmly during a conflict.

- Discuss Your Emotional Processes: Talk to your child about how you handle your emotions. For example, "When I feel stressed, I like to take a few minutes to myself to calm down. Then I can think more clearly about what to do next."

- Show Empathy and Compassion: Demonstrate empathy and compassion in your interactions with others. Your child will learn from your example and begin to emulate these behaviors in their own relationships.

4. Addressing Challenges in Teaching Emotional Management

Teaching children to understand and manage their emotions is not without challenges. Children may struggle to express their feelings, resist learning new strategies, or experience setbacks. It's important to approach these challenges with patience and perseverance.

A. Dealing with Resistance

Some children may resist learning about emotions or using the strategies you teach them. It's important to remain patient and persistent in your efforts.

- Start Small: Begin with small, manageable steps. For example, focus on helping your child recognize and label their emotions before moving on to more complex skills like problem-solving.

- Use Positive Reinforcement: Reinforce any progress, no matter how small, with praise and encouragement. Positive reinforcement can help overcome resistance by making the learning process more rewarding.

- Make It Fun: Incorporate games, stories, and activities that make learning about emotions fun and engaging. This can help reduce resistance and make the process more enjoyable for your child.

B. Addressing Setbacks

Setbacks are a normal part of learning, especially when it comes to managing emotions. Children may regress or struggle with certain aspects of emotional regulation, and it's important to handle these setbacks with understanding and support.

- Be Patient: Understand that setbacks are a natural part of the learning process. Offer patience and support as your child works through these challenges.

- Discuss the Setback: Talk with your child about what happened and how they can approach similar situations differently in the future. This reflection can help them learn from the experience and continue to grow.

- Stay Positive: Focus on the progress your child has made rather than the setback. Encourage them to keep trying and remind them that learning to manage emotions is a journey.

C. Seeking Support

If you're struggling to teach your child about emotions, don't hesitate to seek support. Whether through counseling, parenting classes, or talking with other parents, getting help can provide you with the tools and encouragement you need.

- Counseling: Consider working with a counselor to help your child develop emotional regulation skills. A counselor can provide personalized guidance and support as your child learns to manage their emotions.

- Parenting Classes: Parenting classes focused on emotional intelligence and child development can offer valuable insights and strategies for teaching your child about emotions.

- Support Groups: Joining a support group for parents can offer a space to share experiences, gain insights, and receive encouragement from others who are also teaching their children about emotions.

Teaching children to understand and manage their emotions is one of the most valuable gifts a parent can give. By helping your child develop emotional intelligence, you equip them with the tools they need to navigate the complexities of life with confidence and resilience.

Through strategies like helping children recognize and label their emotions, teaching emotional awareness and triggers, developing healthy emotional expression, equipping children with coping strategies, teaching problem-solving skills, and building empathy, you lay the foundation for your child's emotional well-being.

Creating a supportive environment, reinforcing positive behaviors, leading by example, and addressing challenges with patience and perseverance further strengthens your child's ability to manage their emotions effectively. Remember that teaching emotional management is a journey, and every step you take brings your child closer to becoming a well-adjusted, emotionally intelligent individual.

As you continue to guide your child in understanding and managing their emotions, celebrate their progress and support them through challenges. Your efforts will have a lasting impact, helping your child grow into a resilient, empathetic, and emotionally healthy adult.

Creating a Supportive Environment

Developing a Home Environment That Encourages Open Communication and Emotional Intelligence

A supportive home environment is crucial for nurturing emotional intelligence and fostering open communication among family members. When children feel safe and understood at home, they are more likely to develop the skills they need to manage their emotions and build healthy relationships. This chapter explores how to create a home environment that encourages emotional intelligence and open communication, providing practical strategies for parents to implement in their daily lives.

1. The Importance of a Supportive Home Environment

A home environment that prioritizes emotional health and open communication sets the stage for positive relationships, emotional resilience, and overall well-being. Children learn how to navigate their emotions, express themselves, and interact with others based on the experiences and examples they encounter at home.

A. Emotional Safety

Emotional safety means creating a space where all family members feel secure in expressing their thoughts and feelings without fear of judgment, ridicule, or punishment. It is the foundation of a supportive home environment.

- Validation: When children's emotions are validated—meaning acknowledged and accepted—they learn that their feelings are important and worthy of attention. This validation fosters a sense of security and self-worth.

\- Non-Judgmental Listening: A supportive environment is one where children can share their emotions and experiences without being judged. This approach encourages open communication and helps children feel understood.

B. Open Communication

Open communication involves creating a home atmosphere where all family members feel comfortable discussing their thoughts, feelings, and concerns. It is essential for building trust, resolving conflicts, and promoting emotional intelligence.

\- Regular Dialogue: Encouraging regular conversations about emotions, experiences, and thoughts helps normalize discussions about feelings and reduces the stigma around expressing emotions.

\- Active Listening: Listening actively to what children say—without interrupting or immediately offering solutions—shows that their perspectives are valued and helps build trust.

C. Encouraging Emotional Intelligence

Emotional intelligence involves the ability to recognize, understand, and manage one's own emotions, as well as the ability to empathize with others. A supportive home environment actively promotes the development of these skills.

- Modeling Emotional Regulation: Children learn how to manage their emotions by observing how their parents handle their own feelings. Demonstrating healthy emotional regulation provides a powerful example for children to follow.

- Teaching Emotional Vocabulary: Helping children develop a robust emotional vocabulary enables them to articulate their feelings more accurately, which is a key component of emotional intelligence.

2. Strategies for Developing a Supportive Home Environment

Creating a supportive home environment requires intentional actions and consistent practices. The following strategies can help parents foster open communication and emotional intelligence in their children.

A. Establishing Family Values and Rules

Family values and rules provide a framework for behavior and communication within the home. These guidelines help ensure that the home remains a supportive and emotionally safe space for everyone.

- Identify Core Family Values: Work with your family to identify core values that you all agree are important, such as respect, honesty, kindness, and empathy. These values should guide all interactions within the home.

- Set Clear Communication Rules: Establish rules around how family members should communicate with each other. For example, rules might include speaking respectfully, not interrupting when someone else is talking, and using "I" statements to express feelings.

- Reinforce Values and Rules Consistently: Consistency is key to making sure that values and rules are followed. Gently remind family members of these guidelines when conflicts arise or when someone is struggling to communicate effectively.

B. Encouraging Regular Family Meetings

Family meetings are a powerful tool for promoting open communication and emotional intelligence. They provide a structured time for discussing family matters, resolving conflicts, and checking in with each other emotionally.

- Schedule Regular Meetings: Hold family meetings on a regular basis, such as once a week or once a month. Choose a time that works for everyone and make it a routine.

- Create a Safe Space for Discussion: During family meetings, ensure that all family members feel safe to express their thoughts and feelings. Use active listening, validate each person's perspective, and avoid judgment or blame.

- Address Both Practical and Emotional Topics: Use family meetings to discuss practical matters, such as chores and schedules, as well as emotional topics, such as how everyone is feeling and any challenges they may be facing.

- Encourage Participation: Make sure that everyone, including children, has a chance to speak and contribute to the discussion. This encourages a sense of ownership and responsibility within the family.

C. Building Strong Parent-Child Relationships

A strong, positive relationship between parents and children is the cornerstone of a supportive home environment. This relationship is built on trust, mutual respect, and open communication.

- Spend Quality Time Together: Regularly set aside time to engage in activities that your child enjoys. Whether it's playing games, going for a walk, or simply talking, quality time strengthens your bond and opens the door for deeper communication.

- Show Interest in Their Lives: Take an active interest in your child's daily experiences, friendships, and interests. Ask open-ended questions about their day and listen attentively to their responses.

- Be Available and Approachable: Let your child know that you are always available to talk, whether they have something exciting to share or need help with a problem.

Being approachable helps children feel comfortable coming to you with their concerns.

- Practice Empathy and Understanding: When your child is upset, practice empathy by acknowledging their feelings and trying to understand their perspective. This fosters emotional connection and encourages them to share their feelings more openly.

D. Creating a Routine That Supports Emotional Health

Daily routines provide structure and predictability, which are important for emotional security. By incorporating practices that promote emotional health into your family's routine, you can create an environment where emotional intelligence can flourish.

- Mindful Mornings: Start the day with a calming, mindful activity, such as deep breathing, stretching, or setting a positive intention for the day. This sets a peaceful tone and helps everyone approach the day with a calm mindset.

- Emotional Check-Ins: Incorporate regular emotional check-ins into your daily routine. For example, ask your child how they're feeling at breakfast or during the drive home from school. These check-ins help normalize conversations about emotions.

- Bedtime Reflection: End the day with a reflective practice, such as discussing what went well during the day, what challenges were faced, and what everyone is grateful for. This helps children process their emotions and end the day on a positive note.

- Incorporate Relaxation Practices: Encourage activities that promote relaxation and emotional well-being, such as reading, listening to music, or spending time outdoors. These activities help reduce stress and create a peaceful home environment.

E. Teaching and Reinforcing Emotional Intelligence Skills

In addition to modeling emotional intelligence, it's important to actively teach and reinforce these skills through everyday interactions and specific activities.

- Use Teachable Moments: Everyday situations offer countless opportunities to teach emotional intelligence. For example, if your child is upset about a disagreement with a friend, guide them through the process of identifying their emotions, considering the other person's perspective, and finding a resolution.

- Practice Emotional Labeling: When emotions arise, help your child identify and label their feelings. For example, "It looks like you're feeling frustrated because you can't get your toy to work. Let's take a break and try again later."

- Role-Playing Scenarios: Use role-playing to practice emotional intelligence skills, such as empathy, conflict resolution, and emotional regulation. This can be a fun and effective way for children to learn how to handle different situations.

- Positive Reinforcement: Reinforce emotional intelligence skills with positive feedback. For example, praise your child when they express their emotions calmly, show empathy toward others, or successfully resolve a conflict.

F. Encouraging Independence and Problem-Solving

Encouraging children to solve problems independently fosters confidence, resilience, and emotional intelligence. By guiding them through the process, you help them develop the skills they need to manage their emotions and navigate challenges on their own.

- Guide, Don't Solve: When your child faces a problem, resist the urge to solve it for them. Instead, guide them through the problem-solving process by asking questions like, "What do you think you could do in this situation?" or "What might happen if you try that solution?"

- Encourage Critical Thinking: Help your child think critically about their options by discussing the potential consequences of different actions. This encourages them to consider the impact of their choices on themselves and others.

- Support Risk-Taking: Encourage your child to take reasonable risks and try new approaches to solving problems. Whether it's standing up for themselves in a social situation or trying a new hobby, taking risks helps build confidence and resilience.

- Celebrate Effort and Growth: Focus on the effort your child puts into solving problems and learning new skills, rather than just the outcome. Celebrate their growth and progress, even when things don't go perfectly.

3. Addressing Challenges in Creating a Supportive Environment

Creating and maintaining a supportive home environment is an ongoing process that may come with challenges. It's important to approach these challenges with patience, flexibility, and a commitment to continuous improvement.

A. Dealing with Resistance to Open Communication

Some children may be hesitant to open up or may struggle with expressing their emotions. It's important to be patient and provide gentle encouragement.

- Create Low-Pressure Opportunities: Provide opportunities for communication that don't feel forced or formal. Casual conversations during car rides, walks, or while doing activities together can make it easier for children to open up.

- Be Patient and Consistent: Building trust and open communication takes time. Be consistent in your efforts to engage with your child and show them that you're there to listen whenever they're ready to talk.

- Respect Their Boundaries: If your child isn't ready

to talk about something, respect their boundaries and let them know that you're available whenever they're ready. Forcing a conversation can make them feel uncomfortable and less likely to open up in the future.

B. Navigating Conflicts and Emotional Outbursts

Conflicts and emotional outbursts are inevitable in any family. How you handle these situations can either reinforce a supportive environment or undermine it.

- Stay Calm: When conflicts arise, remain calm and composed. Your ability to stay calm will help de-escalate the situation and model healthy emotional regulation for your children.

- Address the Behavior, Not the Emotion: It's important to distinguish between the emotion and the behavior. While emotions like anger are natural, how they are expressed can be problematic. Address any inappropriate behavior (like yelling or hitting) while acknowledging the underlying emotion.

- Use Conflicts as Learning Opportunities: After the situation has calmed down, revisit the conflict with your child. Discuss what happened, how it could have been handled differently, and what they can learn from the experience.

C. Balancing Emotional Support with Discipline

Providing emotional support while maintaining discipline can be challenging, but it's essential for creating a balanced and supportive home environment.

- Set Clear Expectations: Make sure your child understands the expectations and consequences associated with their behavior. Clear expectations help children understand the boundaries within which they can express their emotions.

- Use Discipline as a Teaching Tool: Discipline should be viewed as an opportunity to teach, not just to punish. When your child breaks a rule, use the situation to discuss what happened, why it was problematic, and how they can make better choices in the future.

- Remain Consistent: Consistency in discipline is key to maintaining a supportive environment. Children need to know that the boundaries and expectations are stable and that the consequences of their actions are predictable.

- Provide Emotional Support During Discipline: While enforcing consequences, also offer emotional support.

Let your child know that you still care about them and that everyone makes mistakes. This combination of support and discipline helps children learn and grow while feeling secure in your love.

4. Maintaining a Positive and Supportive Home Environment Over Time

Creating a supportive environment is not a one-time effort but an ongoing process that requires attention and care. By regularly assessing and adjusting your approach, you can maintain a positive and emotionally healthy home environment for your family.

A. Regularly Assessing the Home Environment

Take time to regularly assess the emotional climate of your home. Consider how well your current practices are working and whether any adjustments are needed.

- Check in with Family Members: Ask your family members how they feel about the current home environment. Are they comfortable expressing their emotions? Do they feel heard and supported? Use this feedback to make any necessary changes.

- Reflect on Your Own Behavior: Reflect on how your behavior contributes to the home environment. Are you modeling the behaviors you want your children to learn? Are there areas where you can improve?

- Make Adjustments as Needed: If you identify areas that need improvement, be willing to make adjustments. This might involve changing routines, implementing new strategies, or seeking outside support.

B. Staying Flexible and Adaptable

Family dynamics change over time, and what works today may not work tomorrow. Stay flexible and adaptable in your approach to creating a supportive environment.

- Adapt to Developmental Changes: As your children grow and develop, their emotional needs and communication styles will change. Be prepared to adapt your strategies to meet these evolving needs.

- Stay Open to New Ideas: Be open to trying new approaches and strategies for fostering emotional intelligence and open communication. What works for one child or situation may not work for another, so flexibility is key.

C. Continuing Education and Growth

Continue to educate yourself about emotional intelligence, child development, and effective parenting strategies. Ongoing learning helps you stay informed and equipped to create the best possible environment for your family.

- Read Books and Articles: Keep reading books, articles, and other resources on emotional intelligence and parenting. The more you learn, the better equipped you'll be to support your child's emotional development.

- Attend Workshops and Seminars: Consider attending parenting workshops or seminars that focus on emotional intelligence and communication. These events can provide new insights and practical strategies.

- Seek Support When Needed: If you encounter challenges that you're unsure how to handle, don't hesitate to seek support. Whether through counseling, parenting classes, or talking with other parents, getting help can provide you with the tools and encouragement you need.

Creating a supportive home environment that encourages open communication and emotional intelligence is one of the most important things you can do for your child's emotional development. By establishing family values and rules, encouraging regular family meetings, building strong parent-child relationships, creating a routine that supports emotional health, teaching and reinforcing emotional intelligence skills, and encouraging independence and problem-solving, you lay the foundation for a home where everyone feels safe, understood, and valued.

Addressing challenges with patience, balancing emotional support with discipline, and maintaining flexibility and adaptability ensure that your home remains a positive and nurturing environment over time. By continuously assessing and improving your approach, you can help your children develop the emotional intelligence they need to navigate life's challenges with confidence and resilience.

As you work to create and maintain a supportive environment, remember that the goal is not perfection but progress. Every step you take toward fostering open communication and emotional intelligence brings your family closer to a more harmonious and emotionally healthy life.

CHAPTER 09

LONG-TERM STRATEGIES AND GOALS

Setting Goals: Establishing Long-Term Goals for Managing Anger and Improving Parenting

Effective anger management and parenting require both immediate strategies and long-term goals. While short-term solutions can help address immediate challenges, long-term goals provide a roadmap for sustained improvement and growth. Establishing clear, achievable goals for managing anger and enhancing your parenting skills not only helps you maintain progress but also ensures that you continue to evolve as a parent. This chapter will guide you through the process of setting long-term goals for managing anger and improving your parenting, offering practical strategies for achieving these goals.

1. The Importance of Long-Term Goals in Parenting and Anger Management

Long-term goals serve as a guiding force that keeps you focused on the bigger picture. They help you maintain consistency in your efforts, track your progress over time, and stay motivated even when faced with challenges. In the context of anger management and parenting, long-term goals are crucial for ensuring that you not only address current issues but also foster continuous personal growth and improvement.

A. Creating a Vision for Your Parenting Journey

Before setting specific goals, it's important to create a vision for what you want to achieve as a parent and how you want to manage your anger. This vision will serve as the foundation for your long-term goals.

- Reflect on Your Parenting Values: Consider the values that are most important to you as a parent. These might include patience, empathy, consistency, or open communication. Reflecting on these values will help you identify the qualities you want to embody in your parenting.

- Envision the Relationship You Want with Your Child: Think about the kind of relationship you want to have with your child in the future. How do you want your child to perceive you as they grow up? What kind of role model do you want to be? This vision will guide your long-term goals.

- Consider the Legacy You Want to Leave: Reflect on the lessons and values you want to pass on to your child. Consider how your approach to anger management and parenting will shape the person your child becomes.

B. The Benefits of Setting Long-Term Goals

Establishing long-term goals offers several benefits, both for managing anger and improving your parenting:

- Provides Direction: Long-term goals give you a clear direction, helping you stay focused on what's most important even when faced with distractions or setbacks.

- Encourages Consistency: By setting long-term goals, you commit to a consistent effort over time, which is crucial for developing new habits and achieving lasting change.

- Tracks Progress: Long-term goals allow you to track your progress over time, giving you a sense of accomplishment as you reach milestones and see the results of your efforts.

- Motivates Continuous Improvement: Knowing that you have clear goals to work toward can motivate you to keep improving and learning, even after achieving initial successes.

2. Setting Effective Long-Term Goals

Setting effective long-term goals involves being intentional about what you want to achieve and creating a plan for how to get there. Your goals should be specific, measurable, achievable, relevant, and time-bound (SMART).

A. Identifying Key Areas for Improvement

The first step in setting long-term goals is to identify the key areas where you want to improve, both in terms of anger management and parenting. These areas will serve as the focus of your goals.

- Anger Management: Consider the specific aspects of anger management that you want to work on. This might include reducing the frequency or intensity of your anger, improving your ability to stay calm under pressure, or developing healthier ways to express your emotions.

- Parenting: Reflect on the areas of parenting where you'd like to improve. This could involve becoming more patient, improving communication with your child, being more consistent in setting and enforcing boundaries, or building a stronger emotional connection with your child.

B. Setting SMART Goals

SMART goals are designed to be clear, actionable, and achievable. By setting SMART goals, you create a roadmap for success that keeps you accountable and focused on your objectives.

- Specific: Your goals should be specific and clearly defined. Instead of setting a vague goal like "become a better parent," focus on a specific area, such as "improve communication with my child."

- Measurable: To track your progress, your goals should be measurable. For example, if your goal is to improve communication, you might measure this by the number of meaningful conversations you have with your child each week.

- Achievable: Set goals that are challenging but achicvable. It's important to be realistic about what you can accomplish within a given timeframe, considering your current situation and resources.

- Relevant: Ensure that your goals are relevant to your overall vision for parenting and anger management. Each goal should align with your values and long-term objectives.

- Time-Bound: Set a specific timeframe for achieving your goals. This could be a few months, a year, or longer, depending on the complexity of the goal. Having a deadline helps keep you motivated and focused.

Examples of SMART Goals:

- Anger Management Goal: "Reduce the frequency of my anger outbursts by practicing deep breathing exercises three times a day for the next six months."

- Parenting Goal: "Improve communication with my child by having at least one 20-minute conversation each evening where we discuss their day and feelings, for the next three months."

C. Breaking Down Goals into Actionable Steps

Once you've set your long-term goals, break them down into smaller, actionable steps. This makes the goals more manageable and helps you stay on track.

- Create a Step-by-Step Plan: Outline the specific steps you need to take to achieve each goal. For example, if your goal is to improve communication with your child, your steps might include setting aside daily time for conversation, learning active listening techniques, and practicing empathy.

- Set Milestones: Establish milestones along the way to track your progress. These milestones serve as checkpoints where you can assess how far you've come and what adjustments might be needed.

- Adjust as Needed: Be flexible and willing to adjust your plan as needed. If you encounter obstacles or find that a particular approach isn't working, revise your steps and try a different strategy.

3. Strategies for Achieving Long-Term Goals

Achieving long-term goals requires commitment, persistence, and the right strategies. The following strategies can help you stay on track and reach your objectives.

A. Building Accountability

Accountability is key to staying committed to your long-term goals. By building accountability into your plan, you increase your chances of success.

- Share Your Goals: Share your goals with a trusted friend, family member, or mentor. Regularly updating them on your progress can provide motivation and support.

- Use a Journal: Keep a journal where you track your progress, document your experiences, and reflect on your challenges and successes. Journaling can help you stay focused and motivated.

- Set Regular Check-Ins: Schedule regular check-ins with yourself or an accountability partner to review your progress. Use these check-ins to assess what's working, identify any obstacles, and make necessary adjustments.

B. Cultivating a Growth Mindset

A growth mindset—the belief that abilities and intelligence can be developed through dedication and hard work—is essential for achieving long-term goals. By cultivating a growth mindset, you approach challenges as opportunities for learning and growth.

- Embrace Challenges: View challenges as opportunities to improve and learn. Instead of avoiding difficult situations, approach them with curiosity and a willingness to grow.

- Learn from Setbacks: Setbacks are a natural part of any journey. When you encounter obstacles, take the time to reflect on what went wrong and what you can learn from the experience. Use these insights to adjust your approach and move forward.

- Celebrate Progress: Recognize and celebrate your progress, no matter how small. Celebrating milestones helps reinforce positive behavior and keeps you motivated to continue working toward your goals.

C. Practicing Patience and Persistence

Achieving long-term goals takes time, and it's important to be patient and persistent in your efforts. Progress may be slow at times, but with persistence, you can reach your objectives.

- Be Patient with Yourself: Understand that meaningful change doesn't happen overnight. Be patient with yourself as you work toward your goals, and recognize that setbacks are a normal part of the process.

- Keep Going, Even When It's Hard: There will be times when progress feels slow or when you're tempted to give up. During these moments, remind yourself of why you set your goals in the first place and keep pushing forward.

- Stay Focused on the Big Picture: When challenges arise, it's easy to get caught up in the details and lose sight of the bigger picture. Regularly revisit your long-term vision and remind yourself of what you're working toward.

D. Seeking Support and Resources

You don't have to achieve your goals alone. Seeking support and utilizing resources can provide you with the guidance, encouragement, and tools you need to succeed.

- Counseling or Coaching: Working with a counselor or coach can provide valuable insights and support as you work toward your goals. These professionals can help you navigate challenges, develop effective strategies, and stay motivated.

- Support Groups: Joining a support group for parents or individuals working on anger management can provide a sense of community and shared experience. Support groups offer a space to share challenges, gain new perspectives, and receive encouragement.

- Educational Resources: Continue learning about anger management and parenting by reading books, attending workshops, or taking courses. The more knowledge and tools you have, the better equipped you'll be to achieve your goals.

4. Maintaining Momentum and Celebrating Successes

Maintaining momentum is crucial for long-term success. By staying motivated and celebrating your achievements, you reinforce positive behaviors and keep moving forward.

A. Regularly Review and Revise Your Goals

Long-term goals are not set in stone. As you progress, it's important to regularly review and revise your goals to ensure they remain relevant and achievable.

- Schedule Regular Reviews: Set aside time every few months to review your goals and assess your progress. Ask yourself whether your goals are still aligned with your values and vision, and make adjustments as needed.

- Be Open to Change: As you grow and evolve, your goals may need to change as well. Be open to revising your goals if you find that your priorities have shifted or if you've achieved a goal sooner than expected.

- Celebrate Milestones: Celebrate each milestone you reach, no matter how small. Recognizing your progress helps maintain motivation and reinforces your commitment to achieving your long-term goals.

B. Reward Yourself for Achievements

Rewarding yourself for achieving your goals, or even for making significant progress, is an important part of maintaining momentum. Rewards can provide motivation and make the journey more enjoyable.

- Choose Meaningful Rewards: Select rewards that are meaningful and motivating to you. This could be a special treat, a day off, or a new book or hobby that you've been wanting to explore.

- Celebrate with Others: Share your successes with friends or family members who have supported you along the way. Celebrating together reinforces the importance of your achievements and strengthens your support network.

- Reflect on Your Journey: Take time to reflect on your journey and the progress you've made. Consider how far you've come, what you've learned, and how you've grown. This reflection can provide valuable insights and motivation for future goals.

C. Staying Committed to Lifelong Learning and Growth

Managing anger and improving parenting are lifelong processes. By staying committed to continuous learning and growth, you ensure that you continue to evolve as a parent and as an individual.

- Embrace Ongoing Education: Keep seeking out new opportunities to learn about anger management, parenting, and personal development. Attend workshops, read books, and stay curious about new strategies and approaches.

- Set New Goals: Once you've achieved your initial goals, set new ones that continue to challenge and inspire you. Lifelong growth is about continually striving to be the best version of yourself.

- Mentor Others: Consider sharing your experiences and knowledge with others who are on a similar journey. Mentoring others not only helps them but also reinforces your own learning and growth.

Setting long-term goals for managing anger and improving parenting is a crucial step in creating a positive and nurturing home environment. By establishing clear, achievable goals, breaking them down into actionable steps, and staying committed to your vision, you can make meaningful progress toward becoming the parent you aspire to be.

Remember that achieving long-term goals is a journey that requires patience, persistence, and a willingness to learn and grow. By building accountability, cultivating a growth mindset, seeking support, and celebrating your successes, you can stay motivated and on track to reach your objectives.

As you continue to work toward your goals, keep the bigger picture in mind and stay focused on the positive impact your efforts will have on your life and the lives of your children. With dedication and perseverance, you can create a lasting legacy of emotional intelligence, resilience, and love that will benefit your family for generations to come.

Self-Assessment

Tools for Self-Assessment and Reflection to Track Progress and Make Adjustments

Self-assessment is a powerful tool for personal growth, particularly in the areas of anger management and parenting. By regularly evaluating your progress and reflecting on your experiences, you can identify what's working well, uncover areas that need improvement, and make informed adjustments to your strategies. This chapter explores various tools and techniques for self-assessment and reflection, offering practical guidance on how to use these methods to track your progress and ensure continuous improvement.

1. The Importance of Self-Assessment in Anger Management and Parenting

Self-assessment allows you to take an honest look at your behaviors, attitudes, and outcomes. It provides a structured way to monitor your progress toward your goals, identify patterns in your behavior, and make necessary changes to enhance your effectiveness as a parent and in managing your anger.

A. Benefits of Regular Self-Assessment

- Increased Self-Awareness: Self-assessment enhances self-awareness by helping you recognize your strengths, weaknesses, triggers, and emotional responses. This awareness is crucial for making intentional changes and improvements.

- Informed Decision-Making: By regularly assessing your progress, you can make informed decisions about what strategies to continue, modify, or abandon. This ensures that your efforts are aligned with your goals.

- Continuous Improvement: Self-assessment fosters a mindset of continuous improvement. By reflecting on your experiences and outcomes, you stay motivated to keep growing and evolving.

B. Creating a Routine for Self-Assessment

For self-assessment to be effective, it should be integrated into your regular routine. Establishing a consistent practice of reflection and evaluation helps ensure that you stay on track and make timely adjustments.

- Schedule Regular Reflection Time: Set aside specific times—such as weekly, monthly, or quarterly—dedicated to self-assessment. Consistency is key to maintaining progress and staying focused on your goals.

- Choose the Right Environment: Find a quiet, comfortable space where you can reflect without distractions. A peaceful environment encourages deeper reflection and honesty.

- Use Tools and Resources: Utilize various tools and resources to guide your self-assessment. Journals, questionnaires, and feedback from others can all be valuable in gaining a comprehensive view of your progress.

2. Tools and Techniques for Self-Assessment

There are numerous tools and techniques available for self-assessment. The following methods can help you evaluate your progress, identify areas for growth, and make adjustments as needed.

A. Journaling

Journaling is one of the most effective tools for self-assessment. It provides a space for you to document your thoughts, feelings, and experiences, allowing you to track your progress over time and reflect on your emotional and behavioral patterns.

- Daily or Weekly Entries: Consider maintaining a daily or weekly journal where you record your thoughts, emotions, and experiences. This regular practice helps you stay in tune with your emotional state and track changes over time.

- Structured Reflection Prompts: Use specific prompts to guide your journaling. For example, you might reflect on questions like, "What triggered my anger this week?" "How did I respond to my child's needs?" or "What progress have I made toward my goals?"

- Reviewing Past Entries: Periodically review your past journal entries to identify patterns, track your growth, and assess whether your strategies are working. This retrospective view can provide valuable insights and motivation.

B. Self-Assessment Questionnaires

Self-assessment questionnaires are structured tools that help you evaluate specific aspects of your behavior, emotions, and progress. These questionnaires can be customized to focus on different areas of anger management and parenting.

- Anger Management Assessment: Create or use an existing anger management questionnaire that asks about your triggers, frequency and intensity of anger, coping strategies, and the outcomes of your responses. Regularly completing this assessment can help you monitor improvements and identify areas that need more attention.

- Parenting Skills Assessment: Use a parenting skills questionnaire to evaluate areas such as communication, patience, consistency, and emotional support. Reflecting on your strengths and challenges in these areas can guide your ongoing development as a parent.

- Frequency of Assessment: Decide how often you will complete these assessments—monthly, quarterly, or semi-annually—based on your goals and needs. Regular use of these tools can help you stay aware of your progress and adjust your strategies as necessary.

C. Reflection and Feedback Sessions

Reflection and feedback sessions involve setting aside time to deeply reflect on your progress and, if possible, gather feedback from others who are close to you, such as a partner, trusted friend, or mentor.

- Personal Reflection Sessions: Schedule regular reflection sessions where you think about your recent experiences, challenges, and successes. Ask yourself open-ended questions like, "What have I learned about myself recently?" or "How can I improve my responses to anger triggers?"

- Seeking Feedback: Invite feedback from someone you trust who can offer an outside perspective on your behavior and progress. This person might observe things that you've missed or provide constructive criticism that helps you grow.

- Documenting Feedback: Keep a record of the feedback you receive and your reflections on it. Consider how you can incorporate this feedback into your action plan and what changes might be necessary.

D. Progress Tracking Charts

Progress tracking charts are visual tools that help you see your progress over time. They can be used to monitor specific goals, behaviors, or emotional responses.

- Behavioral Tracking Charts: Create a chart where you track specific behaviors related to anger management or parenting. For example, you might track the frequency of anger outbursts, the number of positive interactions with your child, or the days you successfully used a coping strategy.

- Goal Progress Charts: Use charts to track your progress toward specific goals. For instance, if your goal is to reduce anger outbursts by 50% over three months, you can chart each week's data to see if you're on track.

- Visual Motivation: Progress tracking charts provide a visual representation of your achievements and can be highly motivating. Seeing your progress laid out in front of you reinforces positive behavior and encourages you to keep going.

E. SWOT Analysis (Strengths, Weaknesses, Opportunities, Threats)

A SWOT analysis is a strategic planning tool that can be adapted for personal development. It involves analyzing your strengths, weaknesses, opportunities, and threats in relation to your goals.

- Identify Strengths: Reflect on the strengths you bring to anger management and parenting. These might include qualities like patience, empathy, or problem-solving skills.

Understanding your strengths allows you to leverage them more effectively.

- Recognize Weaknesses: Acknowledge any weaknesses or areas where you struggle. For example, you might have difficulty staying calm in stressful situations or find it challenging to communicate with your child. Identifying weaknesses is the first step toward addressing them.

- Explore Opportunities: Consider opportunities for growth and improvement. This could involve learning new coping strategies, seeking professional help, or taking a parenting course.

- Assess Threats: Identify any threats or obstacles that could hinder your progress. These might include high-stress situations, lack of support, or unresolved emotional issues. Recognizing these threats allows you to plan strategies to mitigate them.

F. Mindfulness and Meditation

Mindfulness and meditation practices enhance self-awareness and can be valuable tools for self-assessment. By cultivating a mindful approach, you become more attuned to your thoughts, feelings, and behaviors, making it easier to reflect on your progress.

- Daily Mindfulness Practice: Incorporate mindfulness into your daily routine, even if it's just for a few minutes each day. Pay attention to your thoughts and emotions without judgment, and observe how you respond to different situations.

- Meditative Reflection: Use meditation sessions as a time for deep reflection on your goals and progress. As you meditate, focus on specific questions or areas of your life that you want to assess.

- Mindfulness Journaling: Combine mindfulness with journaling by writing down your observations after each mindfulness or meditation session. This practice helps you track subtle changes in your emotional responses and behaviors.

3. Making Adjustments Based on Self-Assessment

The insights gained from self-assessment are only valuable if they lead to meaningful action. After each self-assessment session, it's important to use your reflections to make adjustments that will help you continue moving toward your goals.

A. Identifying Areas for Improvement

Use your self-assessment results to identify specific areas where you can improve. These might include behavioral patterns, emotional triggers, or parenting practices that need adjustment.

- Focus on Key Areas: Prioritize the areas that have the most significant impact on your goals. For example, if you've identified that your anger tends to escalate during high-stress situations, focus on developing better stress management techniques.

- Set New Objectives: Based on your assessment, set new objectives or revise your existing goals to address the areas that need improvement. Ensure that these objectives are specific, actionable, and aligned with your overall vision.

B. Developing an Action Plan

Create an action plan that outlines the steps you will take to address the areas identified in your self-assessment. This plan should be practical and realistic, with clear timelines and milestones.

- Actionable Steps: Break down your objectives into smaller, manageable steps. For example, if your goal is to improve communication with your child, your action steps might include scheduling regular one-on-one time, practicing active listening, and learning new communication techniques.

- Timeline and Milestones: Establish a timeline for achieving each step, with milestones along the way to track your progress. This helps ensure that you stay on track and maintain momentum.

- Adjust as Needed: Be flexible and willing to adjust your action plan as you progress. If something isn't working, don't hesitate to try a different approach or seek additional support.

C. Seeking Additional Support and Resources

If your self-assessment reveals areas where you need additional support, don't hesitate to seek out resources that can help you make the necessary adjustments.

- Professional Help: If you're struggling with specific challenges, consider seeking professional help from a therapist, counselor, or coach. These professionals can provide guidance, tools, and strategies tailored to your needs.

- Educational Resources: Look for books, courses, or workshops that address the areas where you want to improve. Continuing to educate yourself ensures that you have the knowledge and skills needed to achieve your goals.

- Support Networks: Connect with support groups or communities where you can share experiences, gain insights, and receive encouragement from others who are on a similar journey.

D. Reinforcing Positive Changes

As you make adjustments and see progress, it's important to reinforce the positive changes you've made. This reinforcement helps solidify new behaviors and ensures that they become lasting habits.

- Celebrate Successes: Acknowledge and celebrate your successes, no matter how small. Recognizing your progress reinforces positive behavior and motivates you to continue striving for improvement.

- Reflect on Growth: Regularly reflect on how far you've come since you started your journey. Consider the challenges you've overcome, the skills you've developed, and the positive impact these changes have had on your life and relationships.

- Continue Self-Assessment: Make self-assessment an ongoing practice, even after you've achieved your initial goals. Continuous reflection and adjustment ensure that you keep growing and evolving as a parent and in managing your anger.

Self-assessment is a critical component of personal growth, particularly in managing anger and improving parenting. By regularly evaluating your progress, reflecting on your experiences, and making informed adjustments, you can stay on track toward your long-term goals and ensure continuous improvement.

Utilize tools such as journaling, self-assessment questionnaires, reflection sessions, progress tracking charts, SWOT analysis, and mindfulness practices to gain a comprehensive understanding of your strengths, weaknesses, and areas for growth. With these insights, develop actionable plans to address challenges, reinforce positive changes, and seek additional support when needed.

Remember that self-assessment is not a one-time activity but an ongoing process that requires commitment, honesty, and a willingness to learn and grow. By making self-assessment a regular part of your routine, you ensure that you continue evolving as a parent and in managing your anger, ultimately creating a more positive, peaceful, and nurturing environment for yourself and your family.

Continuous Improvement

Strategies for Ongoing Growth and Development in Anger Management

Anger management is not a one-time fix but an ongoing process of growth and development. Continuous improvement in anger management involves regularly assessing your progress, learning new strategies, and applying them in your daily life. It requires dedication, patience, and a commitment to personal growth. This chapter explores strategies for maintaining momentum in your anger management journey, ensuring that you continue to grow and develop over time.

1. Understanding the Need for Continuous Improvement

Continuous improvement is the process of consistently working to enhance your skills, behaviors, and emotional responses. In the context of anger management, it means not only addressing immediate issues but also striving to improve your ability to handle anger in all aspects of your life.

A. The Dynamic Nature of Anger

Anger is a complex emotion that can manifest in different ways depending on various factors such as stress levels, life circumstances, and personal triggers. As these factors change over time, so too can your experience of anger. This makes continuous improvement essential for adapting to new challenges.

- Adapting to Change: Life is full of changes—new job pressures, relationship dynamics, or health issues—that can all affect how you experience and manage anger. By committing to continuous improvement, you ensure that you remain equipped to handle whatever comes your way.

- Preventing Regression: Without ongoing effort, it's easy to fall back into old habits or ineffective ways of managing anger. Continuous improvement helps prevent regression by keeping you focused on your goals and growth.

B. The Benefits of Ongoing Growth

Engaging in continuous improvement in anger management offers numerous benefits, including:

- Enhanced Emotional Resilience: Regularly working on your anger management skills builds emotional resilience, enabling you to handle stress and frustration more effectively.

- Improved Relationships: As you become better at managing your anger, your relationships with family, friends, and colleagues are likely to improve. Others will notice and appreciate your ability to remain calm and constructive during conflicts.

- Greater Self-Awareness: Continuous improvement involves regular self-reflection, which deepens your understanding of your emotions, triggers, and responses. This self-awareness is key to making informed decisions and maintaining emotional balance.

2. Strategies for Continuous Improvement in Anger Management

To maintain continuous improvement in anger management, it's important to adopt strategies that support ongoing growth and development. The following approaches can help you stay on track and continue to enhance your anger management skills.

A. Regular Self-Assessment and Reflection

Self-assessment and reflection are foundational to continuous improvement. By regularly evaluating your progress and reflecting on your experiences, you can identify areas for growth and make necessary adjustments.

- Routine Self-Check-Ins: Schedule regular self-check-ins where you assess how well you've been managing your anger. Ask yourself questions like, "What situations have triggered my anger recently?" "How did I respond?" and "What could I have done differently?"

- Reflection Journaling: Maintain a journal where you document your thoughts, emotions, and experiences related to anger management. Use this journal to reflect on your progress, challenges, and the effectiveness of the strategies you're using.

- Identify Patterns: Look for patterns in your triggers, emotional responses, and behaviors. Understanding these patterns can help you anticipate challenges and develop more effective strategies for managing your anger.

B. Continuous Learning and Skill Development

Anger management is a skill that can always be refined and improved. By committing to continuous learning, you can stay up-to-date with new techniques and strategies that can enhance your ability to manage anger.

- Read Books and Articles: Stay informed by reading books, articles, and research studies on anger management, emotional regulation, and related topics. The more you learn, the more tools you'll have at your disposal.

- Attend Workshops and Seminars: Participate in workshops, seminars, or online courses focused on anger management and personal development. These events provide opportunities to learn from experts, practice new skills, and connect with others who are on a similar journey.

- Explore Different Approaches: Experiment with different anger management techniques to find what works best for you. Whether it's mindfulness, cognitive-behavioral techniques, or relaxation exercises, being open to new approaches can enhance your growth.

C. Setting and Revising Goals

Setting specific, achievable goals is crucial for continuous improvement. As you progress, it's important to regularly revisit and revise these goals to ensure they remain relevant and challenging.

- Short-Term and Long-Term Goals: Set both short-term and long-term goals for your anger management. Short-term goals might focus on immediate improvements, such as reducing the frequency of outbursts, while long-term goals could involve developing more advanced emotional regulation skills.

- Regular Goal Review: Periodically review your goals to assess your progress and determine whether any adjustments are needed. If you've achieved a goal, set a new one that pushes you to continue growing.

- Celebrate Milestones: Acknowledge and celebrate your achievements as you reach key milestones. Recognizing your progress reinforces positive behavior and keeps you motivated.

D. Building and Maintaining Support Systems

Support systems play a critical role in continuous improvement. Surrounding yourself with supportive individuals and communities provides encouragement, accountability, and fresh perspectives.

- Engage with Support Groups: Join a support group for individuals working on anger management. Sharing experiences and learning from others can provide valuable insights and foster a sense of community.

- Seek Professional Guidance: If needed, work with a therapist or counselor who specializes in anger management. Professional guidance can help you navigate challenges, refine your strategies, and stay focused on your goals.

- Involve Friends and Family: Let friends and family members know about your commitment to improving your anger management. Their support and feedback can be invaluable as you work to make positive changes.

E. Practicing Mindfulness and Emotional Regulation

Mindfulness and emotional regulation are essential skills for managing anger effectively. Regular practice of these techniques helps you stay calm, centered, and in control of your emotions.

- Daily Mindfulness Practice: Incorporate mindfulness exercises into your daily routine. Simple practices like deep breathing, body scans, or mindful walking can help you stay present and aware of your emotions.

- Emotional Regulation Techniques: Practice techniques that help you regulate your emotions, such as progressive muscle relaxation, visualization, or guided meditation. These tools can be particularly useful in moments of high stress or frustration.

- Mindful Reflection: Use mindfulness to reflect on your emotional experiences without judgment. This practice helps you observe your thoughts and feelings more objectively, making it easier to identify areas for improvement.

F. Adapting to New Challenges and Life Changes

As life changes, so do the challenges you face in managing anger. Continuous improvement requires adaptability and the willingness to adjust your strategies as needed.

- Anticipate Challenges: Stay aware of potential stressors or changes in your life that could impact your anger management. By anticipating these challenges, you can prepare yourself to handle them effectively.

- Adjust Strategies as Needed: Be flexible and open to adjusting your anger management strategies in response to new situations. What worked in the past may need to be modified or replaced with a different approach.

- Learn from Setbacks: If you experience a setback, view it as an opportunity for learning rather than a failure. Reflect on what happened, why it occurred, and what you can do differently in the future.

3. Maintaining Motivation and Momentum

Staying motivated over the long term is essential for continuous improvement. The following strategies can help you maintain momentum in your anger management journey.

A. Cultivating a Growth Mindset

A growth mindset is the belief that your abilities can be developed through effort, learning, and persistence. Cultivating this mindset helps you stay motivated and resilient, even when faced with challenges.

- Embrace Challenges: View challenges as opportunities for growth rather than obstacles. Approach difficult situations with curiosity and a willingness to learn.

- Focus on Progress, Not Perfection: Celebrate your progress, no matter how small, and avoid the trap of perfectionism. Recognize that continuous improvement is about incremental growth over time.

- Learn from Criticism: Be open to constructive criticism and use it as a tool for learning. Feedback from others can provide valuable insights that help you refine your strategies.

B. Visualizing Success

Visualization is a powerful technique that can help you stay focused on your goals and maintain motivation. By regularly visualizing your success, you reinforce your commitment to continuous improvement.

- Imagine Your Ideal Outcome: Spend time visualizing what success in anger management looks like for you. Picture yourself handling difficult situations with calm and confidence, and imagine the positive impact this has on your life and relationships.

- Create a Vision Board: Consider creating a vision board that represents your goals and the person you want to become. Place it somewhere visible to remind yourself daily of what you're working toward.

- Use Affirmations: Incorporate positive affirmations into your daily routine. Statements like "I am in control of my emotions" or "I handle challenges with calm and grace" reinforce your commitment to continuous improvement.

C. Embracing Lifelong Learning

Continuous improvement is a lifelong journey. Embrace the mindset of lifelong learning, where you remain open to new ideas, experiences, and ways of managing anger.

- Stay Curious: Cultivate a sense of curiosity about yourself and your emotions. Ask questions, explore new strategies, and never stop learning about how to better manage your anger.

- Seek New Experiences: Engage in activities or experiences that challenge you and help you grow. Whether it's trying a new hobby, taking a course, or volunteering, these experiences can provide fresh perspectives and opportunities for personal development.

- Reflect on Your Growth: Regularly reflect on how much you've grown and what you've learned. This reflection reinforces your commitment to continuous improvement and highlights the benefits of your ongoing efforts.

4. Overcoming Obstacles

to Continuous Improvement

Continuous improvement is not without its challenges. Understanding common obstacles and how to overcome them is essential for maintaining progress in your anger management journey.

A. Dealing with Setbacks

Setbacks are a natural part of any personal growth journey. How you respond to setbacks determines whether they become stumbling blocks or stepping stones.

- Practice Self-Compassion: When setbacks occur, be kind to yourself. Acknowledge your feelings, but avoid self-criticism. Remember that everyone experiences setbacks and that they are an opportunity to learn and grow.

- Analyze the Setback: Take time to reflect on the setback and identify what contributed to it. Consider what changes you can make to prevent similar setbacks in the future.

- Recommit to Your Goals: After a setback, recommit to your goals and develop a plan for moving forward. Use the insights gained from the setback to refine your strategies and strengthen your resolve.

B. Managing Fatigue and Burnout

Continuous improvement requires sustained effort, which can sometimes lead to fatigue or burnout. It's important to recognize the signs of burnout and take steps to prevent it.

- Prioritize Self-Care: Make self-care a priority in your daily routine. Ensure that you're getting enough rest, engaging in activities that bring you joy, and taking time to relax and recharge.

- Set Realistic Expectations: Avoid setting overly ambitious goals that can lead to burnout. Instead, focus on realistic, achievable goals that allow you to maintain a healthy balance between effort and rest.

- Take Breaks When Needed: If you're feeling overwhelmed, give yourself permission to take a break. Stepping back temporarily can help you regain perspective and return to your anger management journey with renewed energy.

C. Staying Motivated Over the Long Term

Maintaining motivation over the long term can be challenging, especially when progress feels slow or when you encounter repeated obstacles.

- Connect with Your Why: Regularly remind yourself of why you started your anger management journey in the first place. Whether it's to improve your relationships, enhance your well-being, or be a better role model for your children, connecting with your deeper motivations can help sustain your commitment.

- Celebrate Small Wins: Recognize and celebrate small victories along the way. Each step forward is progress, and celebrating these wins keeps you motivated to continue.

- Seek Inspiration: Surround yourself with inspiration, whether it's through reading success stories, connecting with a supportive community, or setting new challenges for yourself. Inspiration helps keep your energy and motivation high.

Continuous improvement in anger management is a journey that requires dedication, self-awareness, and a commitment to personal growth. By adopting strategies such as regular self-assessment, continuous learning, goal setting, and building support systems, you can maintain momentum and ensure ongoing development in your ability to manage anger.

Embrace a growth mindset, visualize your success, and stay open to lifelong learning as you navigate the challenges and opportunities that come with managing your emotions. Remember that setbacks and obstacles are natural parts of the process, and how you respond to them will determine your continued success.

As you commit to continuous improvement, you will not only enhance your ability to manage anger but also create a more positive and fulfilling life for yourself and those around you. Stay focused, stay motivated, and keep growing—your journey toward emotional balance and well-being is a lifelong adventure that will bring lasting rewards.

CHAPTER 10

RESOURCES AND SUPPORT

Books and Articles: Recommended Readings for Further Exploration of Anger Management

Delving deeper into the subject of anger management through books and articles can provide valuable insights, tools, and techniques to help you on your journey toward better emotional regulation and overall well-being. This chapter offers a curated list of recommended readings, including classic works, contemporary guides, and specialized resources, to support your ongoing growth and development in anger management.

1. Classic Works on Anger Management

These foundational texts have stood the test of time and are widely regarded as essential reading for anyone looking to understand and manage anger more effectively.

A. Anger: Wisdom for Cooling the Flames by Thich Nhat Hanh

- Overview: Thich Nhat Hanh, a renowned Vietnamese Zen master and peace activist, offers a deep and compassionate exploration of anger in this book. He presents mindfulness-based techniques for understanding and transforming anger into peace and compassion.

- Key Takeaways: The book emphasizes the importance of mindfulness in recognizing anger as it arises and offers practical steps for calming and transforming it. It also explores the roots of anger, such as suffering and misunderstanding, and provides insights on how to cultivate compassion and empathy in the face of anger.

- Why It's Recommended: This book is a valuable resource for those seeking a holistic and spiritual approach to anger management. Thich Nhat Hanh's teachings are accessible yet profound, making this an essential read for both beginners and those with a longstanding interest in mindfulness.

B. The Dance of Anger: A Woman's Guide to Changing the Patterns of Intimate Relationships by Harriet Lerner

- Overview: In this influential book, psychologist Harriet Lerner explores how women can understand and manage their anger within the context of their relationships. She focuses on the role of anger as a tool for personal growth and change.

- Key Takeaways: The book offers insights into how women's anger is often misunderstood and provides strategies for expressing it in ways that lead to constructive change rather than destructive outcomes. Lerner emphasizes the importance of self-reflection, boundary setting, and communication.

- Why It's Recommended: While the book is geared toward women, its insights are valuable for anyone interested in how anger manifests in relationships. It's particularly useful for those seeking to break free from destructive patterns and develop healthier ways of relating to others.

C. Anger: The Misunderstood Emotion by Carol Tavris

- Overview: Carol Tavris, a social psychologist, provides a comprehensive examination of anger, debunking common myths and exploring the complex ways in which anger influences our lives. The book is a mix of psychology, sociology, and cultural commentary.

- Key Takeaways: Tavris challenges the idea that anger is always harmful and explores when it can be beneficial. She also delves into the psychological and societal factors that shape our understanding of anger and offers practical advice on managing it effectively.

- Why It's Recommended: This book is ideal for readers who want a thorough understanding of anger from a psychological and cultural perspective. Tavris's writing is both informative and engaging, making complex ideas accessible to a broad audience.

2. Contemporary Guides to Anger Management

These modern texts offer practical advice and evidence-based strategies for managing anger in everyday life.

A. The Anger Control Workbook by Matthew McKay and Peter D. Rogers

- Overview: This workbook is a hands-on resource designed to help individuals understand and manage their anger through practical exercises. It's based on cognitive-behavioral therapy (CBT), which is widely recognized as an effective approach to anger management.

- Key Takeaways: The workbook includes exercises that help readers identify their anger triggers, develop coping strategies, and change their thought patterns. It also provides tools for improving communication and problem-solving skills.

- Why It's Recommended: For those who prefer a structured, interactive approach to learning, this workbook is an excellent choice. It allows readers to actively engage with the material and track their progress over time.

B. Letting Go of Anger: The Eleven Most Common Anger Styles and What to Do About Them by Ronald T. Potter-Efron and Patricia S. Potter-Efron

- Overview: This book identifies and explores eleven common "anger styles," or ways in which people express their anger. It provides tailored strategies for each style, helping readers understand and manage their anger more effectively.

- Key Takeaways: By categorizing anger into different styles—such as passive-aggressive anger, explosive anger, and chronic anger—the book offers specific strategies for addressing each type. It also includes exercises for self-reflection and behavior change.

- Why It's Recommended: This book is particularly useful for readers who recognize specific patterns in their anger and want targeted advice on how to address them. It's practical, accessible, and grounded in real-world experiences.

C. The Cow in the Parking Lot: A Zen Approach to Overcoming Anger by Leonard Scheff and Susan Edmiston

- Overview: This book offers a unique blend of Zen philosophy and practical advice for managing anger. It uses simple, relatable scenarios to illustrate how adopting a Zen mindset can help defuse anger in everyday situations.

- Key Takeaways: The authors emphasize the importance of letting go of the need to be right and learning to see situations from a different perspective. The book includes exercises and reflections designed to help readers develop a more peaceful approach to life's challenges.

- Why It's Recommended: This book is ideal for those who appreciate a more philosophical approach to anger management, combined with practical tips. Its light-hearted tone and relatable examples make it an enjoyable and insightful read.

D. The Anger Trap: Free Yourself from the Frustrations that Sabotage Your Life by Les Carter

- Overview: Les Carter, a psychologist specializing in anger management, explores how anger can become a trap that sabotages relationships and personal well-being. He provides strategies for breaking free from destructive anger patterns.

- Key Takeaways: The book addresses the underlying causes of anger, such as unmet needs and unresolved conflicts, and offers practical steps for developing healthier ways of expressing and managing anger. It also includes insights on how to prevent anger from becoming a habitual response.

- Why It's Recommended: This book is particularly useful for readers who feel stuck in negative anger patterns and want to understand the root causes of their frustration. Carter's advice is grounded in both psychology and personal experience, making it relatable and actionable.

3. Specialized Resources on Anger Management

These books and articles focus on specific aspects of anger management, such as dealing with anger in parenting, relationships, or within the context of trauma.

A. Parenting Without Anger: A 30-Day Guide to Becoming a Calm, Patient, and Loving Parent by Karen Lee

- Overview: This book is designed for parents who struggle with anger and want to create a more peaceful and nurturing home environment. It offers a 30-day plan for reducing anger and improving communication with children.

- Key Takeaways: The book provides daily exercises and reflections aimed at helping parents understand the triggers for their anger, develop patience, and adopt more effective parenting strategies. It also emphasizes the importance of self-care and emotional regulation.

- Why It's Recommended: For parents who find themselves frequently frustrated or overwhelmed, this book offers practical, day-by-day guidance for creating lasting change in their parenting approach.

B. Anger Management for Substance Abuse and Mental Health Clients: A Cognitive Behavioral Therapy Manual by Patrick M. Reilly and Thomas H. Shopshire

- Overview: This manual is specifically designed for individuals dealing with both anger issues and substance abuse or mental health challenges. It provides a structured cognitive-behavioral approach to addressing these issues simultaneously.

- Key Takeaways: The manual includes step-by-step instructions for managing anger, as well as worksheets and exercises that help clients identify triggers, develop coping strategies, and prevent relapse into harmful behaviors.

- Why It's Recommended: This resource is particularly valuable for individuals who are managing multiple challenges and need a comprehensive, integrated approach to anger management.

C. Healing the Angry Brain: How Understanding the Way Your Brain Works Can Help You Control Anger and Aggression by Ronald Potter-Efron

- Overview: This book combines neuroscience with practical advice to help readers understand how the brain's wiring influences anger and aggression. It offers strategies for rewiring the brain to respond to stress and frustration in healthier ways.

- Key Takeaways: The book explains the neurological basis of anger and provides exercises for strengthening the brain's capacity for self-control and emotional regulation. It also addresses the impact of trauma on the brain and offers strategies for healing.

- Why It's Recommended: For readers interested in the science behind anger, this book offers a fascinating exploration of how the brain works and how understanding this can lead to more effective anger management.

D. The Relationship Cure: A 5 Step Guide to Strengthening Your Marriage, Family, and Friendships by John M. Gottman

- Overview: While not solely focused on anger, this book by relationship expert John Gottman provides valuable insights into how improving communication can help manage anger and strengthen relationships.

- Key Takeaways: Gottman's five-step program focuses on building emotional connections through better communication, empathy, and conflict resolution. The book offers practical advice for managing anger within the context of relationships and turning conflict into an opportunity for growth.

- Why It's Recommended: This book is ideal for those looking to improve their relationships by managing anger more effectively and developing deeper emotional connections with others.

4. Articles and Online Resources

In addition to books, there are numerous articles and online resources that offer valuable insights and strategies for anger management.

A. "The Science of Anger: How it Affects the Brain and Body" by Dr. Melanie Greenberg

- Overview: This article explores the physiological and psychological effects of anger on the brain and body. It provides a scientific perspective on how anger develops and what can be done to manage it.

- Key Takeaways: Dr. Greenberg explains the connection between anger and the brain's stress response, offering practical tips for calming the nervous system and reducing the impact of anger on overall health.

- Why It's Recommended: For those interested in the science behind anger, this article offers a clear and accessible explanation of the biological processes involved, along with practical strategies for management.

B. "Cognitive-Behavioral Strategies for Anger Management: An Overview" by the American Psychological Association

- Overview: This article provides an overview of cognitive-behavioral techniques that are commonly used in anger management therapy. It offers practical advice for applying these strategies in everyday life.

- Key Takeaways: The article covers key cognitive-behavioral strategies, such as identifying and challenging negative thought patterns, developing coping skills, and practicing relaxation techniques.

- Why It's Recommended: This resource is particularly useful for individuals looking for a concise introduction to cognitive-behavioral strategies for anger management. It's also a great starting point for those considering therapy.

C. "Mindfulness and Anger Management: How Mindfulness Can Help You Control Anger" by the Greater Good Science Center

- Overview: This article explores the role of mindfulness in anger management, highlighting research findings and practical applications of mindfulness techniques.

- Key Takeaways: The article discusses how mindfulness can help individuals recognize early signs of anger, create a pause before reacting, and develop greater emotional awareness and control.

- Why It's Recommended: For readers interested in integrating mindfulness into their anger management practices, this article offers valuable insights and practical guidance.

D. "The Role of Empathy in Anger Management" by Psychology Today

- Overview: This article examines how empathy can play a critical role in managing anger, particularly in interpersonal conflicts. It offers tips for cultivating empathy and using it to defuse anger.

- Key Takeaways: The article explains how empathy allows individuals to see situations from another person's perspective, reducing the likelihood of anger and promoting more constructive responses.

- Why It's Recommended: Understanding the role of empathy in anger management is crucial for improving relationships and reducing conflict. This article provides practical advice for incorporating empathy into daily interactions.

Exploring books and articles on anger management is an essential part of your journey toward emotional regulation and personal growth. The resources recommended in this chapter offer a wide range of perspectives, from classic wisdom to modern psychological techniques, ensuring that you have the tools and knowledge needed to manage anger effectively.

As you continue to develop your anger management skills, consider integrating these readings into your routine. Whether you prefer in-depth books, practical workbooks, or insightful articles, these resources will support your ongoing growth and help you achieve a more balanced and fulfilling life.

Professional Help

When and How to Seek Professional Help for Anger Management Issues

While many people can manage their anger through self-help strategies and resources, there are times when professional assistance becomes necessary. Seeking professional help is a vital step for individuals who find that their anger is impacting their relationships, work, or overall quality of life. This chapter explores when it's appropriate to seek professional help, the types of professionals who can assist with anger management, and what to expect from the process.

1. Recognizing When to Seek Professional Help

It's important to recognize when anger has escalated beyond what self-help strategies can manage. Certain signs indicate that professional intervention may be needed to effectively address anger issues.

A. Signs That Professional Help Is Needed

- Frequent and Intense Anger Outbursts: If you find yourself frequently losing control of your anger, with outbursts that are intense or disproportionate to the situation, it's a sign that professional help may be necessary.

- Impact on Relationships: Anger that consistently damages your relationships with family, friends, or colleagues is a clear indicator that intervention is needed. If loved ones have expressed concern about your anger or if you've noticed a pattern of relationship breakdowns, it's time to seek help.

- Physical Symptoms of Anger: Persistent anger can lead to physical symptoms such as headaches, high blood pressure, or chronic stress. If your anger is affecting your health, professional support can help you manage it more effectively.

- Legal or Workplace Consequences: If your anger has led to legal issues, such as arrests for assault or domestic violence, or has caused significant problems at work, professional intervention is crucial.

- Difficulty in Managing Anger with Self-Help: If you've tried self-help strategies, such as reading books, practicing mindfulness, or using relaxation techniques, and still struggle to manage your anger, professional help can provide more tailored and effective solutions.

B. The Benefits of Early Intervention

Seeking help early, before anger becomes deeply ingrained or causes significant harm, is beneficial. Early intervention can prevent the escalation of anger-related issues and lead to more successful outcomes.

- Preventing Escalation: Addressing anger issues early can prevent them from worsening or becoming more challenging to manage. Early intervention can also reduce the risk of anger leading to legal, financial, or health problems.

- Improving Relationships: Professional help can provide strategies to improve communication and relationship dynamics, preventing anger from damaging important connections.

- Enhancing Emotional Well-Being: Learning to manage anger effectively improves overall emotional well-being, reducing stress and promoting a more positive outlook on life.

2. Types of Professionals Who Can Help

Various professionals specialize in anger management and can offer different approaches depending on your needs and preferences. Understanding the options available can help you choose the right type of support.

A. Psychologists and Therapists

Psychologists and therapists are trained to help individuals understand and manage their emotions, including anger. They often use evidence-based approaches, such as cognitive-behavioral therapy (CBT), to address anger management issues.

- Cognitive-Behavioral Therapy (CBT): CBT is one of the most effective forms of therapy for anger management. It focuses on identifying and changing negative thought patterns and behaviors that contribute to anger. A CBT therapist can help you develop healthier ways of thinking and reacting to anger triggers.

- Psychodynamic Therapy: This approach explores the underlying emotional issues and past experiences that may be contributing to current anger problems. It's particularly useful for those whose anger is linked to unresolved trauma or long-standing emotional pain.

- Dialectical Behavior Therapy (DBT): DBT combines cognitive-behavioral techniques with mindfulness practices to help individuals manage intense emotions, including anger. It's especially beneficial for those who struggle with impulsive anger outbursts.

B. Counselors and Social Workers

Counselors and social workers provide support and guidance for managing anger, often within the context of broader life challenges. They can help with developing coping strategies, improving communication skills, and addressing relationship issues.

- Individual Counseling: Individual counseling sessions focus on helping you understand your anger and develop personalized strategies for managing it. Counselors often use a variety of therapeutic techniques, depending on your needs and goals.

- Family or Couples Counseling: If anger is affecting your relationships, family or couples counseling can be beneficial. These sessions focus on improving communication, resolving conflicts, and developing healthier ways of relating to each other.

- Anger Management Groups: Social workers or counselors may facilitate anger management groups, where you can learn alongside others who are facing similar challenges. Group settings provide additional support and the opportunity to share experiences and strategies.

C. Psychiatrists

Psychiatrists are medical doctors who specialize in mental health and can prescribe medication if necessary. While medication is not typically the first-line treatment for anger management, it can be helpful in certain cases.

- Medication for Underlying Issues: If anger is linked to underlying mental health conditions such as depression, anxiety, or bipolar disorder, a psychiatrist may prescribe medication to help manage these conditions, which in turn can reduce anger.

- Medication for Impulse Control: In some cases, medication may be prescribed to help manage impulsivity and aggression, particularly if these symptoms are severe and not responsive to other treatments.

D. Life Coaches and Anger Management Specialists

Life coaches and anger management specialists focus on practical strategies for managing anger in specific situations, such as the workplace or personal relationships.

- Life Coaching: A life coach can help you set and achieve goals related to anger management, providing guidance, accountability, and support as you work on developing healthier behaviors and habits.

- Anger Management Specialists: These professionals are trained specifically in anger management techniques and can offer targeted programs or workshops designed to help you understand and control your anger.

3. What to Expect from Professional Help

Understanding what to expect from the process of seeking professional help can make it easier to take that first step. Here's an overview of what you can anticipate when working with a professional on anger management.

A. The Initial Assessment

The first step in professional help typically involves an initial assessment, where the therapist or counselor will gather information about your anger issues, history, and goals.

- Discussion of Symptoms: You'll discuss the frequency, intensity, and triggers of your anger, as well as any consequences it has had on your life. This helps the professional understand the scope of the problem and develop a tailored treatment plan.

- Exploration of Underlying Issues: The assessment may also involve exploring any underlying emotional, psychological, or situational factors that contribute to your anger. This could include discussing past traumas, current stressors, or relationship dynamics.

- Goal Setting: Together with the professional, you'll set specific, achievable goals for your anger management journey. These goals will guide the therapeutic process and provide a framework for measuring progress.

B. The Therapeutic Process

The therapeutic process is tailored to your specific needs and may involve various techniques and approaches. Here's what you can generally expect:

- Regular Sessions: Most anger management therapy involves regular sessions, typically once a week, though the frequency may vary depending on your needs and the severity of the issue.

- Homework and Practice: Between sessions, you may be given homework or exercises to practice. These might include journaling, practicing relaxation techniques, or trying new ways of responding to anger triggers.

- Progress Tracking: Throughout the process, your therapist or counselor will help you track your progress, making adjustments to the treatment plan as needed. Regular check-ins ensure that the therapy remains effective and aligned with your goals.

- Confidentiality and Support: Professional help is provided in a confidential and supportive environment. You can discuss your feelings and challenges openly, knowing that your privacy is protected.

C. The Role of Medication

If you're working with a psychiatrist, medication may be part of your treatment plan. However, medication is typically used in conjunction with therapy rather than as a standalone treatment.

Medication as a Supplement: Medication may be prescribed to help manage symptoms that are contributing to your anger, such as anxiety or depression. It's important to view medication as a tool that supports your overall treatment plan.

- Monitoring and Adjustments: If you're prescribed medication, your psychiatrist will monitor your response to it and make adjustments as needed. Regular follow-ups ensure that the medication is effective and that any side effects are managed.

D. Commitment to the Process

Seeking professional help for anger management is a commitment to your well-being and personal growth. Success in therapy requires active participation, openness, and a willingness to change.

- Active Participation: Your engagement in the therapeutic process is crucial. This includes attending sessions regularly, being open to feedback, and actively practicing the techniques you learn.

- Patience and Persistence: Change takes time, and progress may be gradual. It's important to be patient with yourself and stay committed to the process, even when it feels challenging.

- Long-Term Strategies: Professional help often focuses on developing long-term strategies for managing anger, rather than quick fixes. These strategies will become tools you can use throughout your life to maintain emotional balance.

4. How to Find the Right Professional Help

Finding the right professional to help you with anger management is an important step. Here are some tips for choosing a professional who meets your needs.

A. Researching Options

Take the time to research different professionals and the services they offer. Consider factors such as their qualifications, experience, and areas of specialization.

- Check Credentials: Ensure that the professional you choose is licensed and has the appropriate qualifications. For therapists and counselors, look for credentials such as LCSW (Licensed Clinical Social Worker), LPC (Licensed Professional Counselor), or LMFT (Licensed Marriage and Family Therapist).

- Specialization in Anger Management: Some professionals specialize in anger management or have extensive experience in this area. Choosing someone with this expertise can provide more targeted and effective support.

- Read Reviews and Testimonials: If available, read reviews or testimonials from previous clients. This can give you a sense of the professional's approach and effectiveness.

B. Initial Consultation

Many professionals offer an initial consultation, which can help you determine if they are a good fit for you.

- Ask Questions: Use the consultation to ask questions about the professional's approach, experience, and what you can expect from the process. This is also an opportunity to discuss your specific needs and goals.

- Assess Comfort Level: It's important to feel comfortable with the professional you choose. Trust and rapport are key to successful therapy, so pay attention to how you feel during the consultation.

- Consider Practicalities: Consider practical factors such as location, availability, and cost. Ensure that the professional's services are accessible and fit within your budget and schedule.

C. Making the Decision

After your research and consultation, take some time to reflect on your options and make a decision.

- Trust Your Instincts: Trust your instincts when choosing a professional. If you feel confident in their ability to help you and comfortable with their approach, they are likely a good fit.

- Commit to the Process: Once you've chosen a professional, commit to the process. Be open to the journey ahead and trust that with the right support, you can achieve meaningful change in managing your anger.

Seeking professional help for anger management is a courageous and important step toward better emotional health and well-being. Whether you're dealing with frequent outbursts, struggling in your relationships, or simply finding it difficult to manage your emotions, professional support can provide the tools and guidance you need to make lasting changes.

By recognizing when to seek help, understanding the types of professionals available, and knowing what to expect from the process, you can make informed decisions that support your journey toward better anger management. Remember that this is not a sign of weakness, but a commitment to your growth and the well-being of those around you.

With the right professional help, you can develop the skills and strategies needed to manage your anger effectively, improve your relationships, and lead a more peaceful and fulfilling life.

Support Groups

Information on Support Groups and Online Communities for Parents Dealing with Anger

Support groups and online communities can be invaluable resources for parents who are struggling with anger. These groups provide a safe space to share experiences, learn from others, and gain practical strategies for managing emotions. This chapter explores the benefits of joining support groups, the types of support available, and how to find the right group or online community to meet your needs.

1. The Benefits of Support Groups for Anger Management

Support groups offer a unique combination of emotional support, practical advice, and a sense of community. For parents dealing with anger, these groups can provide critical assistance in managing emotions and improving relationships.

A. Emotional Support and Understanding

One of the primary benefits of joining a support group is the emotional support you receive from others who are facing similar challenges. In these groups, members can share their feelings and experiences without fear of judgment, knowing that others understand what they are going through.

- Shared Experiences: Hearing from others who have experienced similar struggles can be incredibly validating. It helps to know that you're not alone and that others have successfully navigated the same challenges.

- Empathy and Compassion: Support groups are built on a foundation of empathy and compassion. Members are encouraged to listen and offer support to one another, creating a nurturing environment where everyone feels valued.

B. Practical Strategies and Advice

Support groups are not just about sharing feelings; they also provide a forum for exchanging practical strategies and advice. Members can learn from one another's successes and challenges, gaining new ideas for managing anger more effectively.

- Learning from Others: Members often share techniques and approaches that have worked for them in managing their anger. This can include specific coping strategies, communication techniques, or ways to de-escalate tense situations.

- Problem-Solving: When faced with a specific challenge, group members can offer suggestions and feedback, helping you to find solutions that you may not have considered on your own.

C. Accountability and Motivation

Being part of a support group can help keep you accountable in your anger management journey. Regular meetings or check-ins provide structure and encouragement to stay on track with your goals.

- Regular Check-Ins: Knowing that you have a regular group meeting can motivate you to stay committed to your anger management strategies. It provides a sense of accountability, as you'll want to share your progress with the group.

- Encouragement and Motivation: Group members often celebrate each other's successes, offering encouragement and motivation to continue making positive changes. This support can be especially important during challenging times.

D. Building a Sense of Community

Support groups help foster a sense of community, which can be particularly valuable for parents who may feel isolated in their struggles with anger. The connections made in these groups can lead to lasting friendships and a strong support network.

- Reducing Isolation: Parenting can be isolating, especially when dealing with anger issues. Being part of a group helps reduce feelings of isolation by connecting you with others who understand your experience.

- Creating Bonds: Over time, group members often form close bonds with one another. These relationships can extend beyond the group, providing ongoing support and friendship.

2. Types of Support Groups for Parents Dealing with Anger

There are various types of support groups available, each offering different formats and focuses. Understanding the options can help you choose the right group for your needs.

A. In-Person Support Groups

In-person support groups offer face-to-face interaction, allowing members to connect on a more personal level. These groups typically meet at a regular time and location, such as a community center, church, or therapist's office.

- Facilitated Groups: Some in-person support groups are facilitated by a professional, such as a therapist or counselor, who guides the discussion and provides expert advice. These groups often focus on structured anger management techniques and strategies.

- Peer-Led Groups: Other groups are peer-led, meaning they are facilitated by group members rather than a professional. These groups may be more informal, focusing on sharing experiences and providing mutual support.

- Workshops and Classes: In addition to regular meetings, some groups offer workshops or classes focused on specific aspects of anger management, such as communication skills or stress reduction techniques.

B. Online Support Groups and Communities

Online support groups and communities offer the flexibility of connecting with others from the comfort of your home. These groups can be particularly useful for parents with busy schedules or those who live in areas with limited access to in-person groups.

- Discussion Forums: Many online communities feature discussion forums where members can post questions, share experiences, and offer support. These forums are typically available 24/7, allowing members to connect at any time.

- Social Media Groups: Platforms like Facebook and Reddit host numerous support groups focused on anger management and parenting. These groups often provide a mix of discussion threads, articles, and resources.

- Video and Chat-Based Groups: Some online groups offer video or chat-based meetings, which allow for more direct interaction. These groups can provide a more personal connection, similar to in-person meetings, but with the convenience of being online.

- Email Support Groups: In email-based support groups, members communicate through regular email updates or newsletters. This format is less interactive but can still provide valuable information and a sense of connection.

C. Specialized Support Groups

Some support groups focus on specific aspects of anger management or target particular populations, such as parents, men, or individuals with co-occurring issues like substance abuse or mental health conditions.

- Parent-Focused Groups: These groups specifically address the challenges of managing anger within the context of parenting. They may offer strategies for handling conflicts with children, managing stress, and improving communication within the family.

- Gender-Specific Groups: Some groups are designed for specific genders, recognizing that men and women may experience and express anger differently. These groups can provide a more tailored approach to anger management.

- Groups for Co-Occurring Issues: For those dealing with anger alongside other challenges, such as addiction or mental health issues, specialized groups offer support that addresses the interplay between these factors.

3. How to Find the Right Support Group or Online Community

Finding the right support group or online community involves considering your specific needs, preferences, and goals. Here are some tips for finding a group that's a good fit for you.

A. Identifying Your Needs

Start by identifying what you're looking for in a support group. Consider the following questions:

- What Are Your Goals? Are you looking for practical strategies for managing anger, emotional support, or both? Understanding your goals will help you choose a group that aligns with your needs.

- Do You Prefer In-Person or Online Interaction? Consider whether you're more comfortable with face-to-face meetings or if you prefer the flexibility of online groups.

- Do You Need a Specialized Group? If you have specific needs, such as being a parent, a single parent, or someone dealing with co-occurring issues, look for a group that caters to those circumstances.

B. Researching Options

Once you've identified your needs, start researching available groups. You can find information through various channels:

- Local Resources: Check with local community centers, churches, or healthcare providers to find in-person support groups in your area. Many communities offer resources specifically for parents and families.

- Online Directories: Websites like the American Psychological Association (APA) or Mental Health America (MHA) often have directories of support groups. You can search by location, type of group, or specific issues.

- Social Media and Forums: Platforms like Facebook, Reddit, and specialized parenting forums often host groups dedicated to anger management and parenting. You can join these groups to participate in discussions and access resources.

- Therapist Referrals: If you're working with a therapist or counselor, ask them for recommendations on support groups. They may know of groups that are particularly well-suited to your needs.

C. Evaluating the Group's Fit

Before committing to a group, consider attending a few sessions to see if it's the right fit for you. Evaluate the following aspects:

- Comfort Level: Do you feel comfortable sharing your experiences and feelings in the group? A supportive and non-judgmental atmosphere is essential for meaningful participation.

- Group Dynamics: Observe how the group interacts. Are members respectful and supportive of each other? Is the facilitator (if there is one) effective in guiding the discussion?

- Relevance to Your Needs: Does the group focus on topics that are relevant to your situation? Are the strategies and advice offered practical and applicable to your life?

- Consistency and Commitment: Consider whether the group meets regularly and if members are committed to the process. A consistent group with engaged members can provide a more stable and supportive environment.

D. Joining and Participating in a Group

Once you've found a group that fits your needs, take the plunge and join. Here are some tips for getting the most out of your participation:

- Be Open and Honest: Sharing your experiences and feelings openly can be challenging, but it's essential for building trust and getting the support you need.

- Listen and Support Others: Support groups are a two-way street. Be an active listener and offer support to other members, just as they do for you.

- Apply What You Learn: Take the strategies and advice you receive in the group and apply them in your daily life. Reflect on your progress and share your experiences with the group.

- Commit to Regular Participation: Regular attendance helps you build connections with other members and ensures that you get ongoing support.

4. Making the Most of Support Groups and Online Communities

To fully benefit from support groups and online communities, it's important to stay engaged and proactive in your participation. Here are some additional tips for making the most of your experience:

A. Set Personal Goals

Before joining a group, set personal goals for what you want to achieve. These could include improving your anger management skills, developing better communication with your children, or simply feeling less isolated in your struggles.

- Track Your Progress: Keep a journal or notes on how you're progressing toward your goals. Use your support group as a place to discuss your achievements and challenges.

- Seek Feedback: Don't hesitate to ask other group members for feedback on your progress. Their insights can be valuable in helping you stay on track.

B. Explore Additional Resources

Many support groups and online communities offer additional resources, such as reading lists, webinars, or guest speakers. Take advantage of these opportunities to deepen your understanding and skills.

- Educational Materials: Look for groups that provide educational materials, such as articles, videos, or books on anger management and parenting.

- Workshops and Seminars: Some groups offer workshops or seminars on specific topics, such as stress management or conflict resolution. These can provide more in-depth learning experiences.

C. Build Connections Outside the Group

If you feel a strong connection with certain group members, consider building relationships outside of the group. Having a trusted friend or accountability partner can provide additional support between meetings.

- Exchange Contact Information: If appropriate, exchange contact information with group members who you feel comfortable with. You can then check in with each other between meetings.

- Organize Social Gatherings: Some groups organize social gatherings outside of regular meetings. These events can help strengthen the bonds between members and create a more supportive community.

D. Be Patient and Persistent

Change takes time, and it's important to be patient with yourself as you work on managing your anger. Support groups can provide ongoing encouragement and motivation to keep moving forward.

- Stay Committed: Even if progress seems slow, stay committed to attending your group and participating fully. Over time, the support and strategies you gain will lead to meaningful improvements.

- Reflect on Your Growth: Periodically reflect on how far you've come since joining the group. Acknowledge the positive changes you've made and the role the group has played in your journey.

Support groups and online communities offer a wealth of benefits for parents dealing with anger, from emotional support and practical strategies to a sense of community and belonging. By finding the right group and actively participating, you can gain valuable insights, make lasting connections, and develop the skills needed to manage your anger effectively.

Whether you choose an in-person group, an online community, or a specialized support network, the key is to engage fully and commit to your growth. With the right support, you can overcome the challenges of anger, improve your relationships, and create a more peaceful and fulfilling life for yourself and your family.

CONCLUSION

SUMMARY OF KEY INSIGHTS FROM PHILOSOPHICAL, PSYCHOLOGICAL, AND THEOLOGICAL ON MANAGING ANGER

Managing anger is a multifaceted challenge that requires a deep understanding of its origins, expressions, and impacts. Throughout this book, we have explored how philosophy, psychology, and theology each offer unique perspectives and tools for addressing anger effectively. As we conclude, let's recap the key insights from these three disciplines that can guide you on your journey toward healthier anger management.

1. Philosophical Insights

Philosophy provides a rich foundation for understanding the nature of anger and how it can be managed through the cultivation of virtues, reflection, and mindful living.

A. The Role of Virtue Ethics

Philosophical traditions, particularly those rooted in virtue ethics, emphasize the importance of cultivating virtues like patience, temperance, and humility to manage anger. Aristotle's concept of temperance, for example, teaches us to find a balanced response between excessive and deficient expressions of anger. By striving for this balance, we can transform anger from a destructive force into a controlled and constructive emotion.

B. Mindfulness and Reflection

Philosophical practices such as Stoicism encourage the use of mindfulness and reflection to gain control over our emotional responses. Stoic philosophers like Seneca and Marcus Aurelius advocated for examining our thoughts and actions, understanding the impermanence of external events, and focusing on what we can control—our own reactions. This reflective practice helps in recognizing the triggers of anger and responding with reason rather than impulse.

C. Practical Application in Daily Life

The practical application of philosophical principles involves integrating these insights into daily routines. Techniques like pausing before reacting, engaging in self-reflection, and practicing gratitude can help in managing anger more effectively. By aligning our actions with our philosophical beliefs, we create a framework for consistent and mindful emotional regulation.

2. Psychological Insights

Psychology offers evidence-based strategies for understanding and managing anger through cognitive, behavioral, and emotional interventions.

A. Cognitive-Behavioral Techniques

Cognitive-behavioral therapy (CBT) is a cornerstone of psychological approaches to anger management. It teaches us to identify and challenge distorted thinking patterns that fuel anger, replacing them with more balanced and rational thoughts. By restructuring our thought processes, we can reduce the intensity and frequency of anger episodes.

B. Emotional Regulation and Stress Management

Psychological approaches emphasize the importance of emotional regulation and stress management in controlling anger. Techniques such as deep breathing, progressive muscle relaxation, and mindfulness meditation help calm the nervous system, making it easier to manage anger before it escalates. Additionally, understanding and addressing the underlying emotions, such as fear or frustration, that contribute to anger can lead to more effective management.

C. Understanding Triggers and Patterns

A key psychological strategy involves identifying and understanding personal triggers and patterns of anger. By recognizing the situations, thoughts, and behaviors that lead to anger, we can develop proactive strategies to avoid or manage these triggers. Self-assessment tools, such as journaling and reflection exercises, are invaluable for gaining insight into these patterns.

3. Theological Insights

Theology provides a spiritual and moral framework for understanding anger, drawing from religious teachings that offer guidance on how to channel anger in constructive and compassionate ways.

A. Biblical Teachings on Anger

The Bible offers numerous teachings on anger, emphasizing the importance of controlling anger and using it in ways that align with righteous living. Passages from Proverbs, Ephesians, and James, for example, highlight the dangers of unchecked anger and the value of patience, forgiveness, and peacemaking. These teachings encourage believers to reflect on their anger in the light of spiritual growth and moral integrity.

B. The Role of Forgiveness and Reconciliation

Forgiveness is a central theme in many religious traditions and plays a critical role in managing anger.

Theological perspectives emphasize that holding onto anger can lead to bitterness and estrangement, while forgiveness fosters healing and reconciliation. By practicing forgiveness, we not only release our own anger but also create opportunities for restored relationships and inner peace.

C. Spiritual Practices for Managing Anger

Spiritual practices such as prayer, meditation, and contemplation are powerful tools for managing anger. These practices help individuals connect with a higher power, gain perspective, and find inner calm. By integrating spiritual disciplines into daily life, individuals can develop a deeper sense of compassion, patience, and self-control, which are essential for managing anger in a way that aligns with their spiritual beliefs.

The journey to managing anger is ongoing and requires a holistic approach that draws on the wisdom of philosophy, the evidence-based strategies of psychology, and the moral and spiritual guidance of theology. By integrating these perspectives, we can develop a comprehensive toolkit for understanding and controlling anger, leading to healthier relationships, improved well-being, and a more peaceful life.

As you continue on this journey, remember that managing anger is not about suppressing emotions but about transforming them into opportunities for growth and connection. With patience, practice, and the right support, you can turn anger into a force for positive change in your life and the lives of those around you.

ENCOURAGEMENT

FINAL WORDS OF MOTIVATION

As you come to the end of this book, it's important to pause and recognize the incredible effort you've already put into understanding and managing your anger. Parenting is one of the most challenging and rewarding roles you'll ever undertake, and it's natural to encounter moments of frustration and anger along the way. The fact that you've taken the time to learn and grow in this area speaks volumes about your commitment to your own well-being and the well-being of your family.

A Journey, Not a Destination

Remember, managing anger is a journey, not a destination. There will be ups and downs, days when you feel in control and others when you don't. But every step you take toward better understanding your emotions and responding more thoughtfully is a step toward a healthier, happier home. Celebrate your progress, no matter how small, and be gentle with yourself when you encounter setbacks. Each day is a new opportunity to practice what you've learned and to continue growing.

Your Efforts Make a Difference

Never underestimate the impact of your efforts. By working on your anger management, you're not only improving your own life but also setting a powerful example for your children. They are watching and learning from you every day. When they see you handling difficult emotions with grace and patience, they learn to do the same. You are teaching them valuable life skills that will serve them well in their own futures. The work you're doing now will have a lasting positive impact on your family for generations to come.

Stay Connected and Seek Support

It's okay to ask for help when you need it. Whether it's turning to a support group, seeking professional guidance, or simply leaning on friends and loved ones, you don't have to navigate this journey alone. Staying connected with others who understand and support your goals can make all the difference. Surround yourself with positive influences, and don't hesitate to reach out when you need encouragement or advice.

A Brighter Future Awaits

As you continue to apply the strategies and insights you've gained, you'll begin to see the benefits in your daily life. Your relationships will strengthen, your home will become more peaceful, and you'll find greater fulfillment in your role as a parent. The road may not always be easy, but it is worth it. Keep your eyes on the brighter future that awaits—a future where anger is no longer a source of conflict, but a powerful tool for personal growth and deeper connection with those you love.

You've Got This

Finally, believe in yourself. You have the strength, wisdom, and perseverance to manage your anger and create the family life you desire. Trust in the process, stay committed to your goals, and know that every effort you make brings you closer to the calm, loving, and supportive environment you want for your family. You've got this—and you're not alone on this journey. Keep going, and know that your dedication is making a world of difference.

With patience, persistence, and love, you will succeed. Here's to a future filled with peace, understanding, and the joy of being the parent you aspire to be.